Though I know none of the mothers here immortalized, I recognize all of them. Their pictures could come from my family album and their pearls of wisdom from my own mother. In these pages, you can smell the cooking, hear the voices, and perhaps experience the incomparable comfort of your mother's presence. If you're lucky enough to still have a mother, make her a gift of this book.

Jan Schakowsky
Member of the United States House of Representatives

They chop fish, they pull pranks, they hide secrets, they cover sofas in plastic. Mothers come to vivid life here in their children's and grandchildren's words. These are expressions of love, tributes to a powerful bond, and heartfelt evocations of mothers in their sometimes quirky, but always real, glory.

Barbara Brotman
Chicago Tribune *Columnist*

Pirkei Imahot

A Celebration of Our Mothers

Also by the JRC Press:

Is God a Cubs Fan?
   by Arnold B. Kanter
   Illustrated by Darlene Grossman
   with Cubs Season Summaries by Sam Eifling

Pirkei Imahot

A Celebration of Our Mothers

JRC Press • Evanston, IL

Editors: Mel Patrell Furman, Carol Kanter,
    Adrienne Lieberman & Lynn Pollack

Design & Production: Darlene Grossman

The first printing of this book was made possible
by a generous donation from Freddi Greenberg
in honor of her mother, Charlotte Greenberg.

Second printing 2001

Published by JRC Press, 303 Dodge Avenue, Evanston, IL 60202
847.328.7678
fax 847.328.2298
www.jrc-evanston.org

Library of Congress Card Number: 2001086321
ISBN: 0-9676415-1-9

Printed in the United States of America

To all of our mothers

Contents

Foreword

What does Judaism teach us about motherhood? We might begin with a quick scan over thousands of years of Jewish history. To be sure, our civilization has been blessed with countless mythic foremothers who have birthed us and nurtured us over the centuries:

- *Sarah Imeinu*—Sarah our mother and the mother of the Jewish people.
- *Devorah*—Deborah the great judge, political and military leader, referred to in the Bible as *Em Yisrael*—Mother of Israel.
- *Ima Shalom*—Mother of Peace, the great teacher and peacemaker from Talmudic tradition.
- *Glückel of Hameln*—the indomitable single mother of twelve and author of an astonishing medieval German memoir.

On a deeper level, we might say that motherhood itself is a sacred enterprise. Indeed, the Hebrew word for compassion—*rachamim*—comes from the root word for *womb. HaRachaman,* one of God's names, suggests that God's love for humanity is somehow inseparable from a mother's love for her children.

To be a mother thus means to serve as part of a timeless and holy tradition—and it is to this tradition that *Pirkei Imahot* is ultimately dedicated. The remarkable contributions in this book can be read on many levels: as memoirs, as love letters, as thank-you notes, as tributes. But in the end, I believe these writers are participating in a profoundly spiritual endeavor. Together they have created a new kind of sacred text. By introducing us to their mothers, they allow the face of *HaRachaman*—the Compassionate One—to shine out and touch us deeply.

The Jewish Reconstructionist Congregation is honored to share these sacred stories with you.

Harachaman hu yishtabach l'dor dorim,
v'yitpa'ar banu l'netzach netzachim.

Compassionate One, praised by each generation to the next, take pride in us always.

—Rabbi Brant Rosen

Introduction

A beloved portion of the Talmud offers us beliefs and values in
the form of *Pirkei Avot, The Sayings of the Fathers. Pirkei
Avot* is ancient wisdom, indeed. But it's only half the story.
Missing are *Pirkei Imahot, The Sayings of Our Mothers.*

To fill this gap, I convened a committee with a mission:
to gather the wisdom of the warm, loving, aggravating, three-
dimensional women who were our mothers. Our committee
of ten members of the Jewish Reconstructionist Congregation
printed in the January 2000 synagogue bulletin this call for
submissions:

> **Your Mother Wants You to Read This Right Now!**
> *Whistler painted his. Portnoy complained about his.*
> *Oedipus married his. Anna Jarvis immortalized hers*
> *when she started Mother's Day. We've all had*
> *mothers, and some of us have even been lucky*
> *enough to have known grandmothers or other*
> *mother figures. Now we propose to celebrate these*
> *women in a collection called "Pirkei Imahot: A*
> *Celebration of Our Mothers."*
>
> *Not a book of solemn praise, we're aiming instead*
> *for a mixed bag of memories, advice, and anecdotes*
> *that will tickle readers as well as teach them. The*
> *completed book could serve as a JRC fund-raiser that*
> *would make your mother kvell.*

So what can you do? Send us neatly typed
snippets of maternal lore to be considered and
perhaps edited for inclusion in the finished book. The
possibilities are limitless, but if you're stumped for a
topic, how about:
  - *advice on making friends, cooking, falling in*
    love, having children, having grandchildren, etc.
  - *funny or sad stories*
  - *favorite sayings*
  - *spiritual lessons*
  - *things you want to remember*
  - *things you've tried to forget*
Out of this mishmash, believe it or not, we'll make a book!

And, with much work and love, we did. The collection you
hold was inspired by all the women who mothered us. In other
important ways, this book was a group effort. Thank you
especially to the many congregants whose thoughtful, heartfelt
contributions made this publication possible. These are the
stories and pictures you have permitted us to share, and we
thank you for your trust.

Our Rabbi, Brant Rosen, gave us his encouragement and
an eloquent foreword. Book publishing was not in his job
description, but he rose gracefully to the task. Congregational
President Ken Ross and the members of the JRC Board of
Trustees gave us their blessing, figuratively speaking. JRC Vice
President of Communications, Dale Good, served as liaison to
our printer; Syd Lieberman, master storyteller, set our pieces in
order; Diane Melnick, experienced teacher and copy writer,
proofread and copy-edited; Jeff Winter, Associate Professor of
Education at National-Louis University wrote the glossary.

Thank you, too, to the special women who were the work force behind this project. Kudos to the *Pirkei Imahot* Committee: to Judith Blaustein, Carol Ellegant, Ellen Kenemore, Gerry Salzman, and Ruth Wenger, who were there from beginning to end. You attended meetings, waded through intra-committee emails, and volunteered to do whatever needed doing. Your guidance and encouragement were invaluable.

Four committee members also served as editors: Mel Patrell Furman, Carol Kanter, Adrienne Lieberman, and Lynn Pollack. You helped shape the vision. You polished the pieces and returned to us with gems. These pages are shining examples of your talent, hard work, and dedication.

Finally to you, the reader: we invite you, also, to participate in the process of remembering and recording. Perhaps this book will inspire you to write your own stories, poems, essays or letters and to share them with those you love. Or maybe you will pass this book along and encourage a loved one to write. We consider this collection not a finished product, but rather, a work in progress.

Time passes and lives change. But a mother's influence transcends the years to become a part of who we are. A word, an object, a story, a song, a picture, can trigger memories and close the gap of time. We can see our mothers and hear them as clearly as we did yesterday.

We *re-collect.* Recollection links the generations in each of our own personal and family histories. This book, this collection of recollections, may be a link to our greater humanity. In that spirit, we share these offerings with you.

—Darlene Grossman
Project Coordinator

*Sallie Gratch with her mother, Helen Grunsfeld Eichengreen,
and her older sister, Ann, c. 1940*

Sylvia's Funeral

by Lesley Williams

My mother always knew how to turn any occasion into an event. Case in point: Sylvia's funeral.

Sylvia was a goldfish, you see. My mother and her cousin Joy won Sylvia at a carnival and promptly forgot about her, until the morning they found her floating, head down, near the top of her bowl. Chastened at their neglect, Joy and Mom scooped Sylvia out with a tea strainer, laid her reverently in an empty matchbox, and contemplated their loss.

The phone rang: one of Mom's duller boyfriends. Did she want to catch a show that evening? "Oh I couldn't possibly," Mom exclaimed, mouthing her disgust to Joy. "You see . . . umm, Sylvia just died."

A hushed tone on the other end of the line. "I'm, I'm so sorry. I had no idea. Was it sudden?"

"Yes, yes . . . very sudden," Mom replied solemnly, stifling her giggles. "So of course you understand why I couldn't possibly go out."

"Well, do you need anything? If there's something I could bring?"

"Oh, I don't know," Mom sighed, overcome with emotion. "I'm just not myself today. Perhaps . . . if you feel like it, you could bring over a little of that Scotch you like, and . . ." Joy was emphatically waving the empty soda spritzer, "Oh yes, and maybe some soda?"

"Scotch and soda? You got it, baby. I'll be over in less than an hour."

Mom and Joy were still howling with laughter when the phone rang again. This time, it was one of Joy's beaux.

"Dancing? Tonight? Oh my dear, you must not have heard. You see, Sylvia passed away today." Silence, then, "Yes, yes, she was very young . . . it just doesn't seem fair, does it?" Joy managed to extravagantly wipe away a tear while rolling her eyes.

"You know, Doris and I are having a small gathering tonight in Sylvia's memory, if you want to come over. Nothing fancy, we just don't feel up to cooking." A long sigh escaped Joy's lips as she struggled to master her grief.

"You'll bring us a deli tray? Oh, Tom, how thoughtful! Yes, we'll see you at seven o'clock."

And so the evening went. Word spread through the grapevine, condolences were extended, offers of food and drink met with heartfelt acceptance. By eight o'clock the apartment on 47th Street was crammed with somber well-wishers. All bearing gifts, all concerned, all just a little perplexed.

You see, their friends knew that Joy and Mom each had one sister, but no one knew both their names. Joy's friends assumed my Mom's sister had died, and Mom's friends assumed that Joy's had. But did Mom and Joy clear up the confusion? No, they reveled in it, warmly squeezing hands, reluctantly accepting morsels of chicken pressed on them by worried boyfriends, sighing plaintively into their Scotch glasses over the fleeting nature of life.

Naturally, none of their friends would be gauche enough to ask who Sylvia was. But Willis, a relative of one of Mom's suaver beaux, a country cousin just up from the South, couldn't stand the uncertainty any longer. "Hey!" he whispered to a smooth-looking young lady seated next to him, "Who was Sylvia, anyway?"

She glared at him in disdain. "You mean you didn't know Sylvia?"

"Heck no, baby, I just got here yesterday. She must have been something, the way y'all are bawling your eyes out over her."

The young lady sniffed. "Well, I never actually met Sylvia, but I hear she was Doris's older sister and a very promising dancer."

"Oh, no," interjected a friend of my mother's, who had overheard. "That's Berniece. Wasn't Sylvia Joy's younger sister, the teacher?"

"Joy's sister? No, that's Edwina." By now, a small knot of people had gathered around this fascinating, illicit conversation. Cousin Willis was not deterred.

"Well, if she wasn't Joy's sister, and she wasn't Doris's sister, then WHO WAS SHE?" A ghastly silence followed this outburst. Mom and Joy had just re-entered the living room after storing a delicious pâté in the fridge. They looked on in shock.

"You mean," Mom could barely choke out the words, "you don't know who Sylvia was?" Twenty chagrined heads shook. Mom and Joy exchanged mournful glances. Joy cleared her throat. "Would you like to see Sylvia?"

Twenty mouths gaped, twenty throats gulped. Slowly, Mom and Joy turned and walked towards the bedroom, as twenty pairs of eyes followed in fascinated horror. Slowly, the cousins returned, bearing in their outstretched hands—a matchbox.

Stunned, the mourners contemplated Sylvia's remains, then turned to her bereaved next of kin. Mom and Joy had not quite broken character, yet their suppressed hilarity bubbled dangerously near the surface. Mom caught Willis' eye and winked.

Suddenly Willis began to chuckle, to snort, to roar with laughter, despite the miffed looks of the other guests. "They said I'd see some mighty strange things up North," he gasped, "but never in all my born days did I expect to be funeralizing a FISH!"

Joy's lips began to twitch. The suave boyfriend grinned and slapped cousin Willis on the back. Even the smooth young lady had to join in the general laughter. Mom and Joy were promptly forgiven, the Scotch flowed, the pâté and chicken salad were duly consumed, and Sylvia's funeral turned into one of the liveliest parties Joy or my Mom could remember. Or my Dad. For as cousin Willis says, "I knew at once that life with your mother would always be exciting. Anyone who could con a bunch of high-toned city folk into giving a free party for a goldfish was okay with me."

I'm sure Sylvia would agree.

Lessons Learned from Grandma

by Douglas Heifetz
Stephen Heifetz
Jodi Kanter &
Wendy Snell

*Written and delivered in honor of
her eighty-fifth birthday,
February 13, 2000*

Jodi: If you love someone, meet their plane.

Stephen: Try to be an adventuresome eater.

Wendy: Stock the cabinets with your guests' favorite cereals and the freezer with their favorite desserts.

Doug: Provide for the togetherness of those you love.

All: MAKE RESERVATIONS.

Jodi: Respect your intellect and nourish it.

Stephen: There are no worries that can't be put to bed with a bread, butter, and sugar sandwich.

Wendy: You're never too old or too young to learn.

Doug: Wear a tie.

All: MAKE RESERVATIONS—WELL IN ADVANCE.

Jodi: Wear a little lipstick.

Stephen: Own a tie (and maybe some slacks).

Wendy: Pull your hair back; you look so pretty that way.

Doug: Have a lifelong love and partner.

All: BE A LITTLE EARLY FOR YOUR RESERVED TIME.

Rae Waltuch Nussbaum with granddaughters,
Jodi and Wendy Kanter, June 1973

Jodi: Next to family, the dearest thing in life is a good friend. And if that good friend just happens to have an outdoor pool . . .

Stephen: Swim often.

Wendy: Treat in-laws (mothers-in-law, fathers-in-law, sons-in-law, grandchildren-in-law) like your own.

Doug: Travel with a tie.

All: WHEN TRAVELING, BE A LOT EARLY FOR YOUR RESERVED TIME.

Jodi: Adjusting to change is hard, but with patience, determination, and creativity, it's possible—even rewarding.

Stephen: Drive cautiously.

Wendy: Admire your spouse.

Doug: Welcome strangers to our country. Learn from them as you offer what you have to give.

All: CARRY CHICKLETS, WATCH BIRDS.

Doug: You should really wear a sport jacket with that tie.

Tradition

by Barbara Israelite

I never thought of her as a mother-in-law or as Bea or as
Beatrice. She was, from the beginning, Mom. Mom thought
of family—immediate, extended, and adopted—as a truly holy
concept. From the moment we met, I felt welcome and, over
the years, embraced by her love.

I carry many memories of Mom deep in my heart: being at
the lake in Minnesota, dropping by her house in Skokie with
three small children for nurturing, sitting outside in her beautiful
garden or at her kitchen table talking and pasting green stamps
in S&H books. We shared a taste for chicken soup, grits,
mystery books and collecting. And some Passover many years
ago, Mom and I started making gefilte fish together.

There was no recipe for the making of this specialty of hers.
We would start with stock in two of the largest and heaviest
cast-iron pots I had ever seen, let alone lifted. We'd taste and
season the stock many times, then let it simmer while preparing
the fish. We would clean the bones and ready the fish heads for
stuffing; place the fish in a *hock shisel* (a large wooden bowl);
and chop it with Mom's red-handled metal cleaver, which I still
have. We carefully would lay out seasonings and eggs on a dish
towel, the eggs still in their cardboard container. As we'd use an

Bea Israelite, mother-in-law of Barbara, 1980

egg, the empty shell would go back into the egg carton. After all, how else could we tell how many we had used?

You had to get a feel for the fish, adding a little *matzoh* meal, a little pepper, a little salt, a little sugar, a little water, a little onion, some carrots and an egg. You could tell what was needed next by how dry the fish felt, how shiny it was, and how *poochy* (light) it felt. And you had to put your finger into the raw fish to grab a little taste for seasoning. Not too scientific. There was, after all, some magic to this.

We'd plunge into a state of deep concentration in order to remove all the fish bones from the stock. Then we'd shape and count each fish ball and gently drop it into the stock, one fish ball from Mom and then one from me. Not once did our final count ever equal the number of balls that ended up in the pot.

We would spend the whole day with the fish and with each other, starting early in the morning. By noon we were always so hungry that we would fry up a little of the raw fish to make fish patties for lunch. We would sit and talk as we ate, putting off as long as we could the humongous task of cleaning up. What warmth and love we shared. And what a delicious smell filled the house. Each year after the fish was cooked, we would taste it, hug and smile, and pronounce it "the best fish ever."

After Mom died I couldn't make fish for a long time. We had had eighteen years together (not a meaningless number in Judaism) to share, to laugh, to love and be loved. But I wanted more. So a few years ago, I reinstated the tradition. Now just before Passover each year, I share a special day of making gefilte fish with my cousin Sharran. I know Mom would approve.

Nonna's Purse

by Mel Patrell Furman

From the grandmother of my soul I learned that there is no
practical limit to a grandmother's purse. If it started to rain,
she had those folding rain bonnets given out by banks many
years ago, and she carried enough of them for the whole
family. After years as a professional seamstress, she never left
home without a scissors, needle, and thread in case a repair
was needed on the road. A collapsible cup was always kept in
her purse. She carried bottled water—because you never know
if the tap water is really clean where you are. At home she
would boil tap water, cool it overnight, and refill her plastic
bottle in the morning. If anyone got a splinter, she had a
tweezers. She toted bandaids, aspirin, sunscreen, moisturizer.
She also carried a little *Blue Book*. This was a calendar from
the Hebrew Immigrant Aid Society, which had helped her get
settled when she arrived in America and supported her until
she got a job sewing bridal gowns. Thus, she was always
prepared to answer questions about upcoming Jewish holidays
and family birthdays. And, of course, the purse held the *de
rigueur* brag book containing pictures of every living relative
and quite a few dead ones as well.

Laura Tann, grandmother of Boris Furman, 1983

The grandmother of my soul was Nonna, my husband's maternal grandmother, an Italian who had gotten through wartime Europe on her wits, emerging triumphant in America with her daughter and second husband. Nonna's purse was a symbol of that triumph, of all that she—the daughter of a well-to-do family, schooled in art, music, and foreign languages—had learned from getting by in the ugly and chaotic world of Europe in the 1940s. Any item might be tinged with the residue of some horrific experience that had made her understand the need for it. These experiences were never mentioned. The refined world she had abandoned to become an immigrant went undescribed. Her intellectual interests were evident only in the books she carried around, most of them in Italian or German. That bottomless purse almost always held a book, lest she have some time to kill.

Traveling with Nonna made it clear that her purse was also emblematic of her whole way of being. In 1995, a couple of months after losing her husband, Nonna vacationed with us on Cape Cod, where despite her bereavement and dislocation, she was sunnier than the seashore, perennially helpful, showing me snippets of Italian cooking and teaching my kids a bit of Italian.

With a gargantuan effort that left her panting, she climbed down the sand dune to the beach in the morning and back up to the cottage in the afternoon to hang towels up to dry in the fresh air. When we tackled a bike trail, she would drive with us to the trailhead and sit in a folding chair with a book while we rode, enjoying the sun and the salt air, apparently content to be left out of our active jaunts. Evenings, in a cabin without TV, we'd play cards and board games and practice our Italian, reciting the months of the year, counting to ten, and naming the days of the week.

Nonna simply loved caring for her family and being the person everyone could count on when they needed some little thing. Those relationships—with her husband and daughter, her grandchildren and her great-grandchildren—were the glory of her life. When I was brought into my husband's family, who were none too happy to have me, Nonna was loving and welcoming. The trust her kindness inspired in me fostered a wonderful relationship that lasted twenty years, until she died in 1997. She taught me that relationships, attachments, and loves are all we have to fight for. Nonna and her lesson live on in my family.

When we went to Boston to unveil her tombstone, Nonna's grandchildren and their spouses spent the weekend cleaning out her house, going through dozens of photo albums, many framed needlepoints, and piles of greeting cards. It was a bittersweet task. When we finally got to the cemetery, my husband pulled out a small velvet bag he had found during our housecleaning. Another purse of hers, it held everything we needed for a graveside service—kippot and lace head coverings for women; tiny prayer books containing the Mourners' *Kaddish,* which Nonna had collected from funerals of family friends; and a few of those little travel-size packages of tissues.

Frances Frank Nussbaum with great-granddaughter, Jodi Kanter, June 1973

Three Poems

by Angela Allyn

My Two Grandmothers

Rose,
Boy was she something
Mad as a Hatter
She left over three hundred
Hats,
Feathered, furred, flowered
In brilliant colors.
She used to tell people—
And when her mind started to go
She believed—
She was the Ambassadress from Romania
Or was it Hungaria.
Her namesake, my daughter, is THEATRICAL.
By contrast there is
Jane,
Who likes shoes.
And her highballs.
Bourbon
In a tumbler
Never wears hats
Blue shoes, especially
in shades of aqua

She lives in the Midwest but
Her mind
Is in Florida
She was the high school librarian
And I get my love of reading from her.
And I
have many shoes
and many hats.

The Art of Mothering

Squeezed out
from two sets of chickenpox
six sleepless nights
spread haphazardly over two weeks
while mundane details
pile up on pallets
outside, the hours passing.
Some days, you just get through
Without grace.
Picking up
Washing up
Wiping up
Climbing up another flight of stairs
on knees whispering
Osteoarthritis.
Thinking:
This mothering is a younger woman's game.
Keeping going with another cup
of reheated coffee—if I can remember
where I left it, stopping
on the landing
to watch the sunlight dance
in beams with the house dust.
Some days, you just get up
And then you go to bed
without accomplishing anything
on the list
because
you read five picture books

got out all the instruments
put the instruments away
practiced piano
did a load of laundry, twice, because
    the dog threw up on it
put two loads of dishes in the washer and got the
    plates away
before someone bounced them
made juice
cleaned up spilled juice
got out the swimming pool
filled the swimming pool
emptied the swimming pool
made breakfast, lunch, and dinner
gave two squirrely children baths with shampoos
    and brushed out the tangles
read five more picture books
And called your mother
who raised twice as many children and
    is still alive.
She never got anything done
either.

Naptime

The day is lazing towards eveningfall
The air is still
The children nap
Sprawled naked around the house
Mothers with their feet up
Take a breath
Take a solitary pee
Take their own peace—a nap
Read a chapter—
Gathering that final ounce of courage
To face the dinner hour
Hour of arsenic and arguments
Hour of what to what to what to make
Again
Before curtains flutter, legs stir
Bright eyes open wide.

Ruth Wenger with son Benjamin Wenger-Markowitz, 1990

My Mother's Roots

by Pamela Cytrynbaum

My mother sinks down on all fours, knee-deep in bark mulch, dried blood meal and a precisely mixed batter of steer and chicken manure. "Your soil is dry, dry, dry," she sing-songs, "nutrients sucked right out. Nothing will grow in this." She's literally up to her elbows in it, kneading the moist mixture into the hardened expanse of dirt she dug up and turned over in the front yard of my new home.

I stand in the kitchen, smearing tears away with muddy fingers. "The sun's trying to peek out," Mom yells out gamely, glancing up at a regulation gray Oregon spring sky. Mom always sees the sun where it isn't. And she's always been a gardener. There has been some glorious horticultural marvel inside and outside every home she has ever lived in. Her mother taught her. She relentlessly tries to teach me.

As a kid I loved helping her. But then I grew up and lost interest. Mom remains intent on rekindling my interest. She has hung exquisite flower boxes outside every apartment I've ever lived in. She organized my entire condo building of hungover yuppies into an army of morning-sun gardening fiends. Every year she sends me window sill herb gardens and mini African violets.

And now here she is digging into the yard of my husband's and my first house in Oregon. I wish I could say it was this amazing time, a matriarchal transfer of knowledge, skill, love and wisdom. My mother's ability to make everything and everyone around her blossom is one of the things I admire and envy most about her. It also greatly reduces my lung capacity.

My husband and I moved to Oregon a couple of years ago. Jeff was a newly-minted Ph.D. who got a too-good-to-pass-up, tenure-track teaching job. I couldn't fathom leaving my family, job, and beloved hometown of Chicago. But it was a career-launching offer and he's the guy for me. Marriage is always a giant leap of faith, right? So we went, uprooting me from my *shtetl* life with family and childhood friends in Chicago to my exiled life in Oregon's lush Willamette Valley where I hate everything and everyone and can't stop crying. I can't find any cool women friends. I'm clinging to my old life with the kind of desperation that makes it impossible to find a new one. It rains nine months of the year. Nobody honks; it's considered impolite. Who cares that it's so green? It all looks the same after a while. Gray and lonely and drizzly.

So my mom comes to visit every few months. She bursts out of the guest room singing Broadway show tunes. She's singin' in the rain while dragging me on yet another hike in yet another lush Oregon forest. She's lugging a sixty-pound bag of potting soil across the driveway. And on this particular visit, she's knee-deep in bark mulch. And I'm so sad and lonely and missing my mother so desperately that whenever she visits, it's just too depressing to really talk. So we don't. She plants. And bosses me around.

This is her first visit to our new house. "You can do the peas, now, Sweetie." I dig two uneven rows, then absent-mindedly dump the seeds. "You're smushing them all together.

They'll suffocate," my mother says, "and your rows are too shallow." So deeper I dig. Out comes every asphyxiated little pea, and back down it plops, exactly two inches apart into my perfectly spaced, perfectly deep, deeply sad two rows of snap peas. The withered, yellow seeds stare up at me with wrinkled winks.

She started off with gloves. She always starts off a gardening attack with gloves, but I've never seen them last longer than three or four scoops into the dirt. "You've got to feel around in it to know what it needs." "I know, Mom," blurts my eye-rolling inner-adolescent.

By the third day of her visit, where once there were only rusty hooks on our backyard wooden fence, there are now hanging baskets overflowing with dazzling fuchsia and deep purple droplets like mini chandeliers. And everywhere you look, you see hot pink geraniums surrounded by cascades of blue lobelia. Where there once was a barren plot of flyaway dirt, now stand tomato starts delicately trellised, and, of course, my rows of peas.

She didn't have time to plant anything in the patch of dirt in the front yard. She dug it up, turned it over and mixed all kinds of stinky things into it. "Maybe you'll do something with it," she said.

My mother's visit ended like all of her visits do. Her green thumbprint obvious everywhere inside and outside the house. Me feeling better, yet somehow worse. Why won't I let her comfort me? Why do I shut down around her? Why is seeing her so painful? If I miss her so much, why don't I take advantage of her visits? What do I want from her, anyway?

A week later my mother sent me a box of gardenia soap with a note that said it took her about five years to adjust each time she moved to a new city for my father's academic jobs.

Bryna Cytrynbaum with daughter, Pamela, 1998

"The key is to make a garden and make a friend. That opens up everything," she wrote.

This was a revelation. I couldn't picture a time when my mother wasn't deeply rooted in her community. She has an incredible network of amazing friends, book groups (they call themselves "Mentalpause"), and tennis teams. "It didn't just happen," she says when I call to ask about it. She was terribly lonely. Hated it. Clung tightly to her old life. Then slowly made a new one.

After this conversation I begin noticing gardens. I walk by the empty patch of dirt my mother brought back to life. It seems sad not to plant something in it. After all, Mom had gone to all that trouble. On a lark I go to the gardening store and buy several small tomato plants, pea plants, eggplant, red onions, cilantro, mint, sweet basil, and two cucumber plants. As per my mother's instructions, I gently squeeze each plant out of its container, pinch apart the tangled roots, dig the holes, pack the dirt over and pat it firmly. I spend the entire afternoon on my knees in the dirt. No gloves. Then I give the whole thing a long drink of water. I stand over it with the hose. It smells good: earthy, musky, sweet. I get a whiff of each herb. I know which ones are which, but I mark them anyway. Mom says write down what you plant. "You think you'll remember but you always forget." I sit for a long time beside my tiny new garden, listening to the water crinkle-sink into the soil.

Grandmother Sarah

by Elliot Zashin

My maternal grandmother Sarah was a diminutive woman,
round-figured and round-faced with wrinkles and short gray
hair that she covered with a kerchief when she went out. To
me, she represented the old country, with her East-European
Jewish accent, her abundant Jewish cuisine, her old-fashioned
glasses and *babushka,* and her ingenuous attitude toward all
things American.

Sarah came to America from Russia, where she had been
apprenticed to a seamstress. She soon married my grandfather,
who grew up in the same *shtetl.* Sarah had two children and
three grandchildren, who seemed to fill her life with pride and
worry.

Stories about her worrying were part of the family lore.
If we were late coming to visit her, she would imagine we
had been killed in a car accident. Whatever anxiety she went
through on these occasions, though, always changed to delight
when we finally arrived safely, her face lighting up. Her own
life experience, surviving the insecurities of Jewish life in
Czarist Russia, may have shaped such beliefs.

In their mid-sixties, my grandparents moved to the suburban
town where we lived and created a new social life for themselves

through the local Jewish Golden Age Club. Whenever I was
home visiting from college, I would drive them to the club.

One afternoon when I arrived to pick them up, my
grandmother said, "Elliot, you really should learn to speak
Yiddish." This suggestion completely puzzled me, an Ivy
League student. The only time I ever had even a momentary
interest in Yiddish was when my parents spoke it to keep
certain subjects secret from my sister and me. I replied,
"Grandma, why in the world would I want to learn Yiddish?"
"Because,"she said with a certain confidence mingled with
concern for my well-being, "when you get old, all the old
people will speak Yiddish." As things turned out, Grandma
Sarah was far more prescient about my interest in *Yiddishkeit*
than I imagined at the time.

Becoming My Mother

by Adrienne Lieberman

Last winter, my mother and I set out to view the holiday
decorations in Sauganash, just as my family did in our 1950
Chevy forty-five years ago. (No other family members were
even remotely tempted to come along.) As we drove around
that neighborhood, laughing at some of the garish displays but
awestruck at the simple beauty of the illuminated trees and
houses, I felt as if I had come full circle.

As a young woman, I often thought, "I'm not like my
mother." Sarah, my daughter, probably feels the same way
right now about me. But as my mother and I grow older, I'm
tickled by our undeniable likeness. In addition to a shared
delight in light shows, we both love mysteries, historical novels,
romantic movies, parades, and brightly colored clothes.

My mother and I had rapid births, the luck of the genetic
draw. And when our children were young, we kept journals
of the noteworthy and funny things they said. What great
reminders these books are now, both of the delightful
quirkiness of kids' takes on life and the dogged persistence
of individual personality traits.

Speaking of quirky, we both toted candy to the movies.
Naturally, this upset me as a child. But later I understood:

Why spend money on a candy bar when you can bring one from home for less than half the price? So in turn, I mortified my children by bringing candy on movie outings. Now, health conscious in middle age, I bring apples and mortify my husband.

When my mother began to need help with grocery shopping, I noticed that her refrigerator held a bowl of baked sweet potatoes to be enjoyed all week. So does mine. And when we pared down her belongings to move her to a retirement home, we discovered the many journals she had kept on trips and adult education classes. In thirty years, my children will probably discover the same things in my house. I hope, too, that when I'm eighty-something, I'll still be schlepping downtown to do volunteer work.

My father, a devout Jew, would be delighted that all four of his children married Jews and go to synagogue. My mother's happy, too, but even in the kosher home she kept for my dad's sake, my mother would occasionally sneak in a paper plate of the "trayf" shrimp cocktail she couldn't resist. A seafood lover myself, I hold the line at keeping shrimp at home in my own refrigerator, but I grant myself dispensation to consider restaurants and friends' houses neutral territory. I know my mother wouldn't mind.

Last summer we couldn't help falling in love with my son's Japanese girlfriend. I suspect my mother shares my feeling that only a conservative Republican would qualify as marrying out of the pale. Zach's dating a Jewish girl now, but I know my mother won't rest easy until we know for sure that she's a liberal. Me neither.

*Herbert and Eleanore Bass, parents of Adrienne Lieberman,
on their wedding day, April 5, 1941*

Bunny

by Jeff Winter

My mother grew up near Milwaukee in an apartment over her father's dental office. Early on, this Jewish girl shed her name Bernalee, for "Bunny." If someone had told Bunny back then that she would one day marry Charles Winter (from a German Jewish family no less), raise five sons, and come to live in an elegant condo overlooking the ocean off Marco Island, she would have said that this is the stuff of dreams.

Bunny's manner of greeting people offers an accurate first impression. Never the passive bystander, she is first to enthusiastically extend her hand in friendship or give a sincere, heartfelt hug to express her joy of living and excitement in being with friends and family. Psychologists say our body language communicates most. If that's so, my mother's welcomes speak volumes about her acceptance and love of others. A cocktail party graphologist once told her that the large loops of her letters indicate generosity.

Perhaps giving to others was Bunny's way to make herself whole. In any event, no visitor to the Winter home left without a full tummy and, if she had her way, a happy heart. Directing the cooking, conversing, and organizing was Bunny, often with a baby in one arm and a couple of relatives in the kitchen

Bunny Winter, mother of Jeff, 1999

trying (a bit too hard) to help. The abundant food, affection, and joyful noise seemed never to stop flowing. My mom turned simple picnics into lavish banquets, and holidays into extended, joyous celebrations of life.

My mother's generosity of spirit extends beyond the culinary. She has made it to every graduation, *bris,* Bat Mitzvah—any occasion when there was celebrating to share or comfort to give. To this day she and my father are there in body and spirit to offer support and love for people in their circle of care. She spends countless hours holding grandchildren on her lap, reading, talking, and teaching— creating precious moments and reminding us that love must be given away to be enjoyed. I trust that my own daughter has been paying attention and will be her worthy protégée.

The talmudic section called *Pirkei Avot* (Lessons from Our Ancestors) poses the question: What is the finest quality a person can exhibit—generosity, friendliness, good will, foresight, or unselfishness? The conclusion: Generosity, for it includes them all (2:13). Surely the rabbis were describing my mother.

Dancing Plates

by Ruth F. Wenger

My mother's philosophy was live and let live. Yet she did more than tolerate others; she was gracious and welcoming to all comers to our busy household.

Unlike today, with kids and parents scheduled up the whazoo with classes and appointments, the six kids in my family mostly hung out all the time doing homework, jumping on beds, sleeping three to a room, and turning cartwheels in the living room. This haven was held together by my mom, who managed to be bookkeeper and secretary for my dad's construction business while she cooked, baked, washed, worked out at the Chicago Health Club (probably with those fat-jiggling machines), belonged to *Hadassah,* the Sisterhood, and the New Citizens Club, and played kaluki with the little Russian ladies.

In child-rearing, my mother believed in leaving people alone, letting them be. At the dinner table, with a thirteen-year age range among the kids, we naturally had a lot of critics. The younger kids and their eating mannerisms were a target for the older ones. The bigger kids picked on those who chewed too loudly, smelled their food, or made wacky food combinations. At any age criticism can be crushing; from a big sister or brother it can be devastating. My mother had an expression which put everyone in his or her place. Perhaps it was from Yiddish. She told each of us very firmly to "dance in your own plate."

In English this expression makes no sense at all. But with us kids it worked magic. Critics were silent, and the loud chewers seemed to quiet down. We all understood that we should be concerned only with the contents of our own plates.

Chaia (Ida) Friedman (third from the right and sole survivor),
mother of Ruth F. Wenger, Wegrów, Poland, 1936

Outside the context of our house on Tripp Street, my mother's command to "dance in your own plates" sounds so silly. But maybe that was the key to my mom's magic. She gave us boundaries and let us experiment on our plates with some abandon.

Can you imagine ketchup in chicken soup? I was one of those kids who would get a taste for one food and eat nothing else. I happened to be on a ketchup run, and I figured that if a little is good, then more is better. You can imagine the faces of everyone at the *Shabbos* table when I kept pouring ketchup into my soup. I was literally saved by "dance in your own plate." I realized on my own that it tasted awful and never did it again.

Unfortunately, when my mom died, we lost our table choreographer. I remember my dad going into a tirade when my sister Tobey wanted mayonnaise with her corned beef. You would have thought she had committed murder. Dad said it was a waste of food if you put white stuff on red meat. He insisted, "Mustard alone, or leave the table." Now those were the days before food fusion. I remember feeling badly for my sister, but I did not dare tell my dad that he had violated the rule of "dance in your own plate." Instead, dad was yelling about mustard, and my sister, teary-eyed, insisted that she liked mayo. All the while I was thinking to myself, "Wouldn't it be nice to see everyone at the table suddenly shrink and twirl on their dinner plates, each to their own tune while in harmony with the rest of the family?"

Not the End of the World

by Anne Goldberg

My Aunt Ida was born in 1906 and didn't marry until 1937. She said that from the time she was twenty-two years old, whenever she was invited for dinner at someone's home, an Eligible Young Man was also invited. Her single status, and the push by her family and friends to change it, became an unwelcome but inescapable theme in her life.

As a result, she never said a word to me about getting married. But on my thirtieth birthday she gave me a card in which she wrote that she envied me turning thirty at a time when turning thirty wasn't the end of the world for an unmarried woman.

The Letters

by Darlene Grossman

It was rainy the day I climbed up the narrow steps to the attic.
I was eleven years old and looking for treasure. Old enough
to know that there was none—nor any secret passageways or
hidden rooms—but young enough to imagine it, nonetheless.

I loved standing there beneath the bare wooden beams and
slats of the roof. Our out-of-season clothes hung on suspended
rods. On makeshift wooden tables lay piles of cardboard boxes
filled with china, papers, books, and toys.

And then in a darkened area tucked under the eastern
slant of the roof, I noticed for the first time a massive, old,
wooden-ribbed trunk. In spite of its big metal latch, it had no
lock, and I easily lifted the top. The trunk was filled with neatly
pressed and folded monogrammed table linens and bedsheets.
Off to one side lay a bundle of old letters. The topmost one
was addressed to my mother, "Miss Anne Eisenmann," at a
Chicago address. It bore a 1939 postmark and the stamp of the
Deutsches Reich. On the back it read, "Lene Sara Eisenmann,
Nördlingen, Deutschland." The note inside was handwritten in
German. Fear and curiosity took hold of me.

With letters in hand, I climbed down the two flights of stairs
to the kitchen. My mother stood at the stove, her back to me.

"Look what I found upstairs," I began. "What are these?" As Mom turned toward me, her gaze dropped from my face to my hand, which held the letters. Eyebrows frowning, she said with a tone of cool detachment, "Put those right back where you found them. Stay out of my things."

My twin sister and I wore matching dresses as we sat in the back seat of our family car. It was September 1952. My father drove us to our first Sunday school class. "You'll learn a lot of things," he began. "You'll learn about Jewish holidays and Jewish people. And later you will hear about the Holocaust. But," he warned, "you must never talk to your mother about that. Never ask her about her family or her childhood. Never."

Growing up, I felt jealous of my friends who had four living grandparents. Nana and Grandpa, my father's parents, were old when we were born and died when we were still young. Unlike our friends, we had no sepia-colored ancestors looking at us from gilded frames, no old brass candlesticks or finely rubbed bureau. We had no family stories, no funny or heroic tales linking the generations. I felt in my bones that we had no connection; we were wayfarers in America, our temporary port.

Of course, my sisters and I were curious. But our father's words rang so clearly we dared not trespass. "Never ask!" So we grew up dancing around the proverbial elephant in the middle of room, the one that everyone sees but no one acknowledges. And we spun a protective web around our mother.

When I was married and a young mother myself, I visited my parents, who wintered in the South. I vowed finally to break the silence. But to all my questions, my mother answered, "I don't remember any more."

While I visited them, a friend of my mother's from her Jewish girls' school near Stuttgart arrived from the West coast. Each woman had come by herself to the United States, married, and raised her children. Now over coffee in the dining area of the bright and cheerful apartment, Ruth and my mother laughed and chattered like young girls. My father and I took a long stroll along the beach in order to give them time to be alone. When I returned Ruth remarked, "It's amazing. She hasn't forgotten a thing. Your mother even remembers her visa number!"

Sixty-five years marked a turning point in my mother's life. One evening after a family dinner, she gathered her four daughters in front of her china cabinet. "Take what you want now," she advised us. I remember looking at the objects behind the glass: a collection of delicate *demitassen*, some little silver spoons and napkin holders, a porcelain basket with flowers, some crystal glassware.

Then I turned slowly to face her. "None of this," I said. "I want the letters." *The Letters.* The letters I'd found in the attic a lifetime ago. The letters we had not mentioned in nearly thirty years. "Oh. I burned them long ago," she said quietly.

Seven years later my mother arrived at our home for the family seder. She came alone. My father and twin sister had died four years earlier. Still looking strong and dignified, Mom set the steaming, heavy bowl of creamed spinach on my kitchen counter. She greeted her eight grandchildren and handed each one a small gift. Then she approached me as I stood by the stove. "And this is for you," she said, giving me a large brown envelope. Written on it were the words, "Ask me." Inside were the letters.

I did ask her several times after that. But I think the silence was too difficult to overcome, and perhaps the pain also. "Not now, Dar," she always responded.

Mom died eighteen months later. I gathered the letters to be translated, and, over the next several months, I received three or four each week. Bit by precious bit, I collected the past and mourned for my mother and the young girl she had been.

Anne and Martin Kramer with twin daughters,
Donna and Darlene, Chicago, July 1947

* * *

Stuttgart, 7 April 1939
Meine liebe Annelies!
In our imagination we all made the big trip with you. I hope after all the stress you will be more relaxed when you receive this letter. . . . Begin your new life bravely in your new home like you left your old home. . . . Deine Mutter

Nördlingen, 20 April 39
Liebe Annelies!
We are happy to know you are on American soil, which is your home now. If just somebody would let us know how you enjoyed the boat trip, your first impression from the other side of the world . . . .

*Did you get our letters? In time we will find out how
much fun it is to learn English. Dein Vatter*

*Esslingen, 1 Mai, 1939
Liebe Liesl!
For the first time you are getting a letter from me,
from Germany! Thanks for the card. I am going to
learn English as fast as I can. . . . I'm sure you still
understand German. Then next time I would like to
write in English. To all hello, Dein Bruder Günter*

* * *

Bericht über das Schicksal der Nördlingener Juden
(Report about the Nördlingen Jews)
*On Easter 1942 the Jewish people under sixty-five
years left with a transport. They left by train with
police to Munich. In the beginning they wrote. By
the end of 1942, they stopped writing. When they
asked for food, all they got was two hundred grams
of watery soup and a little bread. They slept on the
bare floor, and the only clothing they had was what
they wore. Mr. Heinrich Eisenmann did not have to
go along. He was working for a firm which did not
release him. But he did not want his family to go
alone, so he drove to Munich to be with them.*

*In August 1942 all the other Jewish people from
Nördlingen had to leave, first to Augsburg and then
to Theresienstadt. Jewish homes were taken over
by the government. Shortly before April 1945,
Nördlingen was bombarded and the railroad station
destroyed. During the war the temple had been used
for grain storage. The cemetery was demolished,
and even the monuments were stolen.*

Two Poems

by Carol Kanter

Heritage

For Frances Frank Nussbaum

Grandma candied carrots
bought in Kroger jars.
In a pan she'd melt real
butter, add brown and white
sugars in equal parts,
pour in some carrot juice,
heat not quite to boil;
and when it thickened
drizzle the syrup
over the firm (never mushy)
orange cylinders waiting
warm and covered
in a separate heavy-
bottomed pan over a flame
so gentle a kitchen spy
might sneeze it out,
upset the delicate, split-
second timing of her "easy
as falling off a log" magic
that left family taste
buds coated by sweet roots
and her recipe begging
to be handed down.

First published in *Kaleidoscope Ink,* Vol. 8, 1997.

The Keeper Couch

For Mary Fine Waltuch

Well past seventy,
Grandma goes and buys
a couch, swathes its lizard green
and gold upholstery
in tough plastic
to keep it new for her and Pop,
who plan long lives.
In winter the cover leaches
cold through wool pants;
in summer bare thighs
sweat and stick,
so getting up—
no matter how slow—rips
angry like Aunt Olga
shuffling cards when losing
their Saturday night canasta game.

Maybe for special company
or on Passover
with every corner scoured,
she'll take that cover off, nervous
that some bitter herb
or, God forbid, a drop
of Manischewitz
escape the seder table's dust
of matzoh crumbs, find
her naked sofa's satin skin,
stain it and those marks
would always show.

As though she'd ever dare
remove the plastic after that.

When they sell their two-flat,
they move, with couch,
to a ninth floor apartment
too cramped for Passover crowds.
Their insistent children strip
the sofa bare of plastic.
Years after Poppy dies, Grandma
moves to a nursing home where,
until she's a century old,
she tells how she rode
her horse three miles to school,
but never mentions Pop
or that she no longer sees
or how she gave Salvation
Army the couch,
its condition "Excellent."

Gussie Brodsky, mother of Beryl Michaels, 1931

A Premarital Check

by Bob Turner

Two nights before our wedding, on a hot Alabama summer night, my mother-in-law decided to have "the talk" with me that she thought her husband would have had if he had been alive. Sitting down at the dining room table over a couple of glasses of J&B, she started out by wishing us happiness and joy in our lives together. She then had to make sure that we had chosen proper contraception. Never mind that her future son-in-law was already a gynecologist.

Marie-Adele Zimmermann Summers,
grandmother of Sean Egan, c. 1933

Grandmaman

by Sean Egan

From her I inherited the freckles on my shoulders, horrendously ugly toenails, hands that love playing in dirt, and the smirk of a smile instead of a loud guffaw. She lived on an old farm nestled between fields of corn, forests, and gently rolling hills in the Piedmont region of Maryland. The outbuildings of the farm— the huge barn, the garage, the chicken house, and the old springhouse—had fallen into unsalvageable states of disrepair by the time I began spending my summers there. The house, over a hundred years old, never changed from year to year. The pond, at the lowest depression in the property's topography, was referred to as "Mrs. Summers' Bottom." Mrs. Summers was my grandmother.

Grandmaman lived in the modern addition built in the late 1950s. It included a kitchen, bathroom, and one bedroom. The rest of the house was closed off most of the year. She passed through it only to ascend the steep, narrow stairs to forage for old towels in the upstairs linen closet, or to journey to the bowels of the cellar. The cellar frightened me something fierce. It was cold and dank, with a pressed dirt floor and stone walls. She kept bins of potatoes and onions, jars and jars of preserves from the garden, and who knows what all else hidden down in that cellar.

But though I liked nothing else about it, this cellar had one cupboard where Grandmaman stored her raspberry jam. That jam would lure me down. I would consume jars of it during each visit. Then, at my departure, Grandmaman would have me wrap up a few more jars in paper or in my clothes to pack in my suitcase. These I would hide and guard furiously from my siblings once back home.

Marie-Adele Zimmermann Summers, or Grandmaman, had been educated in Switzerland and seemed to know everything—all the classics of Western civilization, opera, world history, the royal families of Europe. She was addicted to the game show "Jeopardy," which she could have won hands tied and blindfolded.

But her succinct lessons about all the small things in life remain most vivid for me. She had emigrated to this country from Switzerland in the 1930s and spoke to me in a mixture of English and French, with a smattering of German and Spanish thrown in. "Use it up, wear it out, make it do or do without" was one of her stock phrases. I think that is why she still wore my deceased grandfather's old cardigans and tennis shoes as she went from one meadow to the next, planting, weeding, collecting, gathering, commenting, building, fixing. "Every-thing has its place and to every place its thing," she would say. That doesn't sound so good in English, but I knew that it meant I should not move her things around. She didn't talk for the joy of hearing herself, so I generally listened when she did.

My mother and I now continue the dialogue that she and her mother used to have: Come spring, what seeds should we buy this season? Who has the best tomato plants? What new fruit bush or tree should we add to the garden or yard? How early do we dare transplant our seedlings into the freshly thawed ground? In the summer and early fall, my mother and I compare notes on the quantity of produce we have harvested. We share ideas on what to do with it all, giving some away, cooking up some for eating immediately, processing some for the cold, dark months of winter. On any given Saturday in fall or winter, I can call my mother and confirm that she, too, has a pot of soup simmering on the back burner of the stove, a concoction of the week's culinary remains.

Grandmaman and Mom and myself, we all like taking care of things ourselves. Nothing breaks that we can't somehow try to repair. Sewing and knitting, making clothes and house linens, they are both *mavens* at this. Me, I'm a little less adept, but I'm not a total *nudnik*. Sewing I can handle. And knitting? My mother was still trying to teach me when we were in Switzerland visiting cousins just last summer. Furniture? No big deal, I'll make it if I can't find something in the alley. Leaf and snow blowers? Are you kidding? That's why we were given two arms, two legs, and yard sales full of other people's old tools and equipment.

But like Grandmaman, Mom and I can walk through a museum of art and not say a word. Savor a fine meal or just enjoy a piece of rich chocolate. Stroll on a beach or through a forest, or maybe spend a morning in the garden, pulling weeds before the bugs get too bad. We don't have to talk to share these pleasures of life.

* * *

Before she passed away, I told my grandmother how much I loved her. Such words were not in her vocabulary: "Of course you love me. Of course I love you. But, *pah!* you don't have to talk about it." Still, I tell my mother how I love her. And I can just hear her saying to herself, as her mother would have, *"Genug,* already."

The Family of Rebecca Rubin, Brooklyn, NY, c. 1907

With Perfect "Emunah"

by Alan J. Goldberg

I practice a meditation in which I visualize returning to an embryonic state. I see myself in the womb with the universe nurturing me, and I remember being completely surrounded by the love of my mother and father. My mother especially gave me this gift of trust in a universe that provides a sense that everything is going to be okay.

She planted this sense of trust in me early. We lived on the third floor of a six-flat on Chicago's West Side, near 13th Place and Independence Boulevard. I was about three years old when my mom sent me on an errand to The Egg Man, in the English basement level of our building. She may have lurked a few steps behind me, but I have always remembered the day that I was first trusted to venture out into the world. Since then, thanks to her, I have always felt that everything is going to be okay.

A Mother's Curse

by Jan Yourist

My family lived in a working-class neighborhood in Ohio, a
neighborhood designed for the workers at the Willys Jeep
plant. We were the only Jewish family for miles around, and
we ended up in the midst of a Catholic enclave.

Mr. and Mrs. Brewer lived on the second floor of the house
next door. They had a small balcony where we would see them
sitting during the late afternoon sipping cocktails. Mr. Brewer
had been a used car salesman but had retired by the time I was
a little girl. Mrs. Brewer always seemed to be in a fog. She
would smile and drift in and out of focus (both ours and hers).

Mr. Brewer was very particular. He worshiped his car, a
Lincoln Continental that he dutifully and lovingly washed and
waxed. If there were nothing more to clean on the exterior or
interior of the car, he would sweep out the garage until, as my
mother would say, you could eat off the floor.

Mr. Brewer was continually perturbed by my brother and
my sister and me because we made a lot of noise and
stomped all over his lawn, which he took great pains to
manicure. He and his landlord put up a fence which ran down
the center of their corner lawn to prevent us from crossing it.

Pearl Yourist, supermother of Jan, 1954

(Seeing that fence in the center of their lawn was my first brush with the surreal.)

Mr. Brewer also had very little love for our cat "America."

One day when he was sweeping out the garage for the third time that week, he called me over. I was scared; Mr. Brewer wasn't one for small talk and usually had some complaint or scolding to deliver.

"Look at what your cat did. Footprints all over the hood of my car. If your cat ever does that again, I will kill him."

The tears welled up in my eyes. Kill America? I believed he would. I ran home. "Mom, Mom, Mr. Brewer is going to kill our cat!"

I watched as my mother swelled with indignation and that proverbial fury of a mother protecting her young. She seemed to grow taller, stand straighter, and transform herself from an

overweight, out-of-shape, make-up-less, wild-haired mom into
a knight in shining armor. Her face glowed; fire lit up her eyes.
She squinted as if deep in thought, then marched out of the
house heading for next door. We scurried after her.

She found Mr. Brewer polishing the hood of his car. She
looked directly into his eyes and said that she heard he had
threatened America.

He looked at her, rag in hand, and said slowly and
purposefully, "You know, Hitler's ovens were not big enough."

At the time I was not sure what he meant by that statement.
It seemed totally out of context and confusing. What did all that
have to do with his car and America?

Deliberately but with great passion, she spoke these words,
emphasizing each of them with a pointed finger directed close
to his face: "IF YOU SO MUCH AS RAISE A HAND TO TOUCH
OUR CAT, MAY YOU DROP DEAD!" With that she walked back
into our house, the rest of us following.

The next morning, an ambulance pulled up at the Brewers.
The paramedics carried Mr. Brewer out on a stretcher. He had
had a heart attack during the night and was dead before he
reached the hospital.

I remember seeing my mother at the kitchen table, her
head in her hands, murmuring, "Jan, do you think I killed
him?" I'm not sure what I answered at the time, but I was
totally and completely convinced that she had.

My mother had become a real superwoman who could
murder with a single pointed remark. In that summer of 1958,
in our despondent neighborhood, our mother had become
invincible. My brother and sister and I felt absolutely safe in the
refuge of her words. Besides, it was clear we shouldn't cross
her. So for the next two weeks, we listened to my mother
without a single argument.

What's in the Middle?

by Charlene Gelber

"What do you want for lunch?" my mother asked me, as usual.

"Anything's fine; I don't care."

I didn't remember seeing deli meats in the refrigerator. But midway through the morning, I began to salivate just thinking about what she might have prepared. Good garlicky salami, maybe on rye, or white bread with enough mustard. Even better, corned beef, definitely on rye, with plenty of mustard. My stomach started making noises. The sandwich I was going to eat for lunch got bigger and better as classes dragged on and on.

The bell! It's lunch!

I raced to my locker, grabbed the greatest meal ever to be packed in a brown paper bag, bought a coke, found my friends, and sat down. I looked at my friends' feeble attempts at hearty school lunches. Mere excuses for sandwiches: Paper-thin bread with a *schmear* of peanut butter and jelly, see-through imitations of deli meats, and, for the unfortunate, the cafeteria's mysterious gray meat.

My lunch: The pickle that had been smelling up my locker all morning, wrapped in aluminum foil so it wouldn't get the bag wet with its wonderful juices; potato chips, to add crunch;

Clara Powitz with daughter Charlene, 1949

a piece of homemade cake; and, with a nod to the food pyramid, an apple. Finally, the crowning glory: The sandwich. I ripped the waxed paper off, revealing two thick slices of bakery rye bread, mustard oozing out of the sides. I took that first bite and floated off into deli heaven. Took a second bite and a third and realized I wasn't tasting salami or corned beef. What was going on here? Did someone, aware of my mother's prize-winning lunches, lift the meat without leaving a trace? Hardly possible.

    I put the sandwich down on its wrapper and hesitantly lifted the top slice of bread. Plenty of mustard, couldn't see the meat. I flipped the sandwich over, lifted the bottom piece of bread and saw more mustard. I pulled the sandwich apart, with a piece of bread in each hand, and saw nothing fall out onto the paper. There was nothing inside this colossal sandwich but air. I had an air sandwich. Where was my longed-for salami or corned beef?

My excitement shifted to embarrassment. What excuses could I make for an air sandwich? Dare I call my mother an airhead? I only wanted mustard? Children are starving in Europe, we sent the meat overseas? What could have been going on in her mind that morning?

Home after school, I asked, "Uh, Ma. Did you forget something in my lunch today?"

"No dear. Why? Didn't you have enough?"

"Ma, the sandwich was only mustard and bread. You embarrassed me."

"Oh, I'm so sorry, Sweetheart. I didn't have salami or corned beef in the house. And besides you said you didn't care."

"But, Ma, it was only mustard and bread. Nothing in the middle."

"No, actually, it was filled with love."

So, for lunch I'd eaten a pickle, chips, cake, apple, bread with mustard and love. And it had filled me up.

Mid-Life Mothering

by Betty Van Leuven

I don't know exactly when I started to breathe easy as a
mother. Somewhere between my oldest child learning to drive
and last child becoming a Bat Mitzvah, I only know I relaxed
considerably. This feeling had less to do with their actual well-
being than it did with a sense of my own vulnerability. I never
did worry much about their physical safety or even their health.
My complacency centered on the knowledge that I was there,
a monolithic force protecting them from any ill wind that might
blow their way. As long as I was alive, they would continue
to thrive.

It's hard to maintain vigilance, though, and as time went
on, I did stop thinking that every fatal disease was out there
hunting for me. I even felt bold enough to take an occasional
plane flight. But the less I worried about me, the more I
began to worry about them. Formerly benign activities and
objects, such as trips to the park and baseball bats, started
to evoke scenes in my mind of havoc and danger. I read up
on childhood leukemias and installed a carbon monoxide
detector in the basement. The benefit was the loss of my
egocentrism, and what a relief that was. What a latecomer
I was to the society of my peers, mothers who had been

anxious for the fate of their children since their birth, with nary a care for their own demise.

My children have grown up, more or less unscathed. And I find, amazing to me, that I am no longer afraid of my own death. Not that I've taken up flying small aircraft or now choose to forego mammograms. But the buoyancy, the lightness of being that comes from knowing that if I disappear tomorrow my children will go on relatively unimpaired, is a wonderful feeling. It almost makes up for all those other middle-age feelings such as regret at not having accomplished enough, and having no control over the inevitable effects of gravity.

Mid-life motherhood often does entail painful separations from one's parents as well as one's children, but what a joy it is to feel, ultimately, so dispensable. So, to those young mothers out there still in the throes of that very appropriate stage of intense succoring and bonding, it's okay to give in to those instincts. Your turn to live dangerously, if that is your heart's desire, will arrive. Should you live so long, and the odds are you will, you can savor the loosening of those silken tethers, and maybe even feel yourself feather light, floating benignly over the lives of your children, content to watch and whisper words of encouragement when the wind is blowing in their direction. You can enjoy the freedom of having outlived the constraints of the biological imperative to produce offspring and shepherd those offspring to an independent state. You will also realize, as all mothers eventually do, that your most strenuous efforts to ensure their safe passage to maturity are, like life itself, totally unpredictable.

Evelyn Mendelson with son-in-law and daughter,
Howard and Carol Ellegant, 1998

Never Too Late

by Carol Ellegant

Mom had never lived alone before. After Dad died, she ended
her year of mourning and, in her annual Rosh Hashanah card,
announced to long-time friends that she had a new fellow in
her life. He was an old family friend whose wife had died a
number of years before. Six hundred miles away, I learned
about her dating less directly. Whenever Mom went to a local
concert or play, suddenly she added a "we" to the description.
When she mentioned getting an invitation to an event or
someone's home, there was a "we." I finally stopped asking
who the "we" was. Mom had always been a rather upbeat
person, but her voice took on fresh delight as she recounted
her week's activities, upcoming events and her fellow's
compliments on her cooking, her clothes and her company.
When he went to Israel and brought her back a necklace, she
was thrilled and wore it every day. It's nice to know that life
can continue to fill with joy past age seventy.

Trash Collector Day

by Jeff Balch

I was the third of three, and after I left for college Mom lived
alone. She remained at the little house, the one we moved to
from the larger house after Dad remarried.

She had become a curious mix of cheeriness and defeat,
kind of a bubbly recluse, a bit of a Tennessee Williams character
in my mind. She bustled in the kitchen, but only for us kids.
She kept working for the county as a probation officer. She did
okay at that, mostly, although she would sometimes fall behind
due to a perfectionism and a blossomy writing style unsuited for
the job. Probationers seemed to appreciate her as one who
cared in a system that did not.

The Monday after she died, I was out front doing some
yard work. It was garbage pick-up day and a young fellow
came up the driveway wheeling a big barrel. "How's Mrs.
Balch doin'?" he asked. I hadn't had to tell a stranger yet.
I took a breath. "Well, she was real sick, and, mm, she died
a couple days ago." I said it as gently as I could.

He was younger than I, with especially young eyes, and
he turned them to the ground trying to find words. "Oh, I'm
sorry," he stammered, and hurried away.

I was looking down too, choked and teary. When I looked up again a few seconds later I saw three men coming across the yard—an older man flanked by the first young fellow and a second. A trash collector committee, I couldn't help thinking. The older one spoke. "Are you Mrs. Balch's son?" he asked, his hand out. We shook and I said yes. "Well," he said, with glances left and right at his crew, "we just want you to know your mom was the nicest person on our route."

Maisie Balch with her children Chad, Trudy, and Jeff, 1987

So We Dance

by Rochelle M. Bernstein

"Watch," she said.

Then she stepped away from the table, held her arms
out to an imaginary partner, and my mother began to waltz.

"Back, side, together. Forward, side, together." She turned
under the arch into the living room. And in tempo to the
three-four rhythm in her imagination she continued, "Watch
me. It's easy. See."

I was four years old when my mother taught me to dance
while we waited for the *Shabbes* chicken to roast up golden
in its brown paper sack. We didn't need the radio to fill the
room with *Roses from the South* or *The Beautiful Blue
Danube*. Wherever my mother was, there was music. She
proudly proclaimed with great truthfulness that she "couldn't
carry a tune in a bucket." So she married a man with a sweet
tenor voice who did a mean rhumba.

She's moving to Chicago to live with me. I'm going
through her kitchen—one step ahead of the movers—trying to
sort out what they can pack and what goes into the trash. For
a woman who now drinks only at weddings, my mother has an
amazing collection of swizzle sticks. Several still carry the

golden impression of the Broadwood Hotel, a place where my mother became slightly scandalous.

During the war, as I heard in stories told around a kitchen table while my mother's sisters made four cups of tea from one tea bag and two lemons, the Broadwood played host to semi-professional basketball games. After the games, the floor was cleared for dancing.

"Your mother," as one sister began it, "danced all night." As the teaspoons stirred, "Everyone wanted to dance with her." Nods around the table. "She never lacked for a partner." At this point there always followed a hushed pause, and the tale resumed almost in a whisper: "A black man asked her to dance, and she danced with him." All eyes slowly turned toward my mother.

She said she never understood what the fuss was about. "He was a very good dancer."

In Chicago, I sit reading. In the midst of all the prose, I see a block of type. Familiar, compact, truncated outline. A new poem by a poet whose name I don't recognize. So, I must read.

After I read the lines, I want to banish them from my memory. Withdraw their shape and mass from my eyes. I'd tear the page out and burn the book if my mother hadn't taught me that destroying a book was heresy. For indulging in the sin of curiosity, I am reminded that this time even Hope has flown away.

Aron Krich's poem, "In the Coffee Shoppe," contains these lines:

And though she sits like a Hadassah *lady*
At a lunch, my mother has become a mouth
As I was at the oral stage. "Food is love."
I feed her strawberry sundae from a spoon.
She tries to eat the paper napkin too.

My mother doesn't eat napkins. She tears them in half, no matter how small they start out. I wince at her frugality. Doesn't she know that I can afford whole napkins? Everything she wants, anything she needs, she'll have. My mother has Alzheimer's disease. I want her to be the woman I've always known. This, of course, changes nothing.

The disease has already changed everything. It's changed our relationship. She knows my voice only on the telephone— a legacy of over twenty years of living in different cities. Day to day, however, I'm either sister, niece, or nephew.

She wonders where he went—the one who was sitting on the sofa just a minute ago. The one she came upstairs to find.

"Where's Eddie?"

"He's not here."

"Maybe it was Dave? I saw him downstairs."

"Eddie's in Philadelphia with Pearl. Both of 'the boys' still live in Philadelphia. You're the one who moved—to Chicago. You must miss them a lot."

"Since when did they live there?" And around a few more times.

"Who am I?" I whisper.

"My sister?"

"I'm your daughter."

"I didn't know I had a child that lived."

Esther Zamochnick Bernstein, mother of Rochelle, c. 1939

My birth, bookended by a still-born daughter and a miscarriage, never took place. The disease steals more than memory. This thief steals joy and consolation.

Before I moved Mom to Chicago, an Orthodox friend—the younger sister I "adopted" years ago—told me I was storing up points for the next world. "It's the greatest *mitzvah* you can do," she said. She knows me well enough to know how little that comforts me. In the manner of younger sisters, she became suddenly profound. "In spite of all the loss, maybe this is the time for her soul to find what it needs to heal." With more than a little arrogance, I told myself that I could provide whatever was needed.

It's nearly a year. I'm not so arrogant any more. And when I can tear myself away from my own anger and grief, I try to look for signs of the things that console my mother in her growing confusion and isolation. Before I've even taken my coat off, we're dancing and laughing to the *klezmer* music.

She has dirt under her fingernails from working in the garden. The man who led the *kiddush* asked her to read some prayers. She smiles and her eyes glisten, "He was so proud of the way I read."

The *klezmer* music reminds her of her parents, and she cries. Her tears remind me how long love lasts. She washes her hands from pulling weeds. She teaches me, again, to be useful in the world and to get satisfaction from the smallest details of life. The *kiddush* blessings return to her lips as if she were showing her father what she'd learned in Hebrew school. How we are related to each other may not matter, after all. Keeping faith with her and with our tradition may be the strongest bond, the greatest consolation.

My mother says she's found a wonderful new partner to dance with at the daycare center. As she talks I see her following the melodies and movements of the waltz. Sometimes, I am reminded, the soul also needs to dance.

Things My Mother Has Taught Me

by Emily Rose

*For my mother, Laurie Kahn,
on her fiftieth birthday, August 9, 1999*

Chasing a dream is okay
as long as you're in shape

Being independent is wonderful
as long as you call home once a week

Spending too much money on a dress
   can be fun
as long as you take a friend along
   for conversation

There is no such thing as loving your family
   too much

Turn your failures into lessons

Fill your house with flowers

Fill your heart with people.

Dear Omi

by Ray Grossman

NOTE: This is excerpted from a letter I wrote to my mother in October 1994, for no particular calendar occasion. I simply wanted to tell her, while she was still going strong, what she has meant to me. Today she is eighty-seven and still spends much of each day taking care of others. She drives people to their cancer treatments, delivers food to disabled people, and works at the Hadassah and hospital resale shops. She still bakes "Omi" cookies for everyone, has Shabbat dinner at her house every other week, shops for her synagogue, and attends Friday night services. And she is learning how to email her grandchildren.

Dear Omi,

You have given me so much for which I am grateful: a safe place to live and grow up in; a house full of love and good food; lots of solid values; caring and encouragement. You taught me about the engine that does. You taught me to be all I could be. You taught me about my father.

I am also grateful for what you have not passed on to me: fear, although you must have had more than your share; hatred, although many were mean to you; impulses to ridicule,

Trudel Grossman, mother of Ray, 1993

to shame, to swear, to blame, to feel sorry for yourself, to wait around for good luck to happen.

I have felt your pride in me, even when I didn't deserve it. You have loved, not judged me. You have loved those I loved. You have blessed the lives of my children, through their knowing you and by linking our generations.

And, in concrete ways, you have always been there to help. I know I must have said countless "thank yous." I want you to know that I remember, even though you never require thanks for anything you've done. Not for that time I was sick after I moved out of your home and you traveled across the city to bring me, what else, but chicken soup. Not for all the performances, games, meets, and graduations you attended for our children. Not for the million or so times you baby-sat. Not for all your chauffeuring.

Over how many centuries have people thought and talked, written and read about love? People long for love, but you spread it. You serve love like those "Omi" cookies you still bake. And we all eat it up.

I just wanted to be sure you knew.

Your loving son,
Ray

confessions of a fabric junky's daughter

by Julia Bena Goldberg

pins and needles obstacles for bare feet headed to bed
lullaby of machine hum as bobbin catches top thread
siblings not of blood or flesh
but foam rubber fake fur wire and mesh
bald bejeweled mannequins grin
room strewn scraps: sparkles glitter sequin
wonderland for child eyes: hot glue gun elastic surger
scissors full-length mirrors cotton rayon velvet Singer
Viking Bernina spray paint leather wigs and lace
pinking shears pattern paper most beloved place
alone in shop surrounded by playmates
midnight ritual lonely playdates
wrap myself matted hair in fuchsia synthetic
threadspool fingers crimson lipstick pathetic
visible now amidst shadows and creatures
who come daytime usurp throne of main feature
stay up late sad but dancing
of Mother's glance and smile romancing

*Ida Feldman, mother of Diane Melnick,
dressed as a gypsy, 1932*

spin and weep
she lay asleep
with dreamtime visions New York City garment district
breath soft and hungry for next fabric fix

WWMD?

by Lynn Pollack

Perhaps you've seen those bracelets some Christian youth wear. Emblazoned with the initials *WWJD* (for "What Would Jesus Do?"), they serve as talismans to help teenagers through difficult times. I have a bracelet of my own. It's an invisible one that I've kept on since my mother died, and it bears these letters: *WWMD* (What Would Marion Do?)

Marion was my mother, a five feet and a half-inch—forget that half-inch at your peril—dynamo of a woman. She terrified half the world with her outspokenness, fearless determination, and ability to make the tough calls. The rest of us just marveled and learned when to stay out of her way.

I first invoked the *WWMD* magic a few months after her death. It's no surprise that the situation involved food. Marion was an ambitious and prolific cook, who claimed to have no love for her Orthodox upbringing but still whipped up dish after dish on Friday afternoon: enough food to last all weekend. Marion's recipes were highly sought after, and she was generally happy to oblige. And though hers were typed, laminated, and in impeccable alphabetic order, her wonderful *mandel brot* recipe mysteriously disappeared after her death, as did her well-used dutch oven. Some say she wasn't so

Marion Pollack, mother of Lynn, 1937

willing to share her secrets, after all.

I was attempting to recreate her famous toffee squares. After three tries, it was clear that I was doing something wrong, even though I'd successfully baked these many times in her kitchen when I lived at home. Then I remembered that I had inherited my mother's cookie sheet, the very tin that had baked hundreds of batches of these delicious cookies. I retrieved it from the cardboard box and plopped the dough on its still shiny and speck-free surface. Suddenly, it was as though my mother's hands were guiding me as I firmly, yet gently coaxed that tricky mixture of brown sugar, butter, and a little flour into place. Naturally, these toffee squares came out perfectly. Determined to keep that pan spotless, I now reserve it for toffee squares alone. Woe be to anyone in my family who considers baking a pizza on it.

Since then, I've invoked my mother frequently, sometimes for far graver matters. I've discovered that several other women—cousins, my best friend since kindergarten—also call on my mother's wisdom to guide them through difficult passages. After all these years, her presence still looms large. In fact, Marion seems to keep growing taller in our memories.

That half-inch isn't all we'll never forget.

My Mother's Three Loves

by Syd Lieberman

My mother was a knockout, with classic good looks that reminded people of Ingrid Bergman. Mom's dark blond hair fell in soft curls around an Eastern European face with high cheekbones. She had blue-gray eyes, full red lips, and eyebrows that were so light she had to pencil them in.

Twenty was an eventful year for Mom. That year she got married and gave birth to her first child. But before that, she got engaged. Twice. Pete Brown, her first fiancé, was one of four brothers who worked at his family's hot dog stand. Nine months after they met, Pete and Mom were engaged. But she never felt quite sure he was the one for her. As it turned out, he wasn't.

Little did Mom know that in the wings a second Prince Charming awaited his audition: my father. "About two months after we got engaged," explained my mother, "Pete decided to go on a two-week fishing trip. I told him not to leave me alone, but he wouldn't listen. And that's when I met Sammy."

My father's sister, Julia, was Mom's girlfriend. Pa was older, a gambler who usually dated only gentile girls. Mom had

A longer form of this piece was published in *Streets & Alleys: Stories with a Chicago Accent* (Little Rock, Arkansas: August House, 1995).

noticed him, of course. He dressed sharply, and his dark good looks carried an air of danger and excitement. For her visit to Julia Lieberman's house that day, my mother wore a black crepe dress with a sheer chiffon top. Like Pete Brown, my mother was fishing. And that day she caught my father.

Pa, an expert dancer, quickly swept her off her feet. As he held her close on the dance floor of the Aragon Ballroom, Pa whispered in her ear, "I'm glad you know how to dance. If you didn't, I couldn't marry you." Pete Brown soon faded to a memory, a fish story about the one she threw back. The night before Pete returned, Pa asked Mom to marry him, and she said yes even though she still wore Pete's ring.

Mom might have made a snap decision to marry my father, and she might have sometimes questioned her gamble on a gambler, but my parents remained married for thirty-five years. Of course, those years changed Mom. You can see the change when you thumb through old photographs. The early photographs show a beautiful woman with wavy hair, a curvaceous figure, and a saucy look on her face. In later photographs she is more matronly: her cheeks have filled out and her smile has softened. In most shots, she's posing at the beach or at the park surrounded by her three young sons. As her sons grow taller, her hair turns platinum blond. In her fifties, she gets plump and dons glasses. Her hairline recedes. By her sixties, she's wearing a blond wig and has begun to resemble the grandmother she is.

But while Mom's appearance changed, her desirability never waned. Nine months after my father died, the second great love of her life, Maury, moved in. Maury had played cards with Pa at the neighborhood card joint in the back of a cigar store. They met a month after Pa's funeral, when he helped Mom home with her groceries. "So we began going places together," said Mom. "Naturally, when his lease ran out, I invited him to stay with me." Maury stayed eleven years.

"Maury was a good man. When Pa died, he left nothing but debts. He'd gambled away everything. But when Maury died, he left me all the money in his two checking accounts. And then one day when I went to make the bed, I flipped the sheets in the air and all these dollar bills started flying around the room. He had kept a hundred dollars tucked between the mattress and the bedsprings and didn't even tell me. It was like his final good-bye."

Three years later, Mom met Wally. She had been manless that whole time, unless you count Mr. Colen. Mom didn't. She had known Mr. and Mrs. Colen for over forty years. After Mrs. Colen died, Mom and Mr. Colen began to keep company. But Mr. Colen's idea of a day out was taking her to the cemetery so they could visit their dead spouses. This made for a peculiar double date.

Mr. Colen was surprised when my mother sent him a birthday card. He couldn't figure out how she had known his birthday. "Of course, I know," she told him. "I've seen it on your tombstone a dozen times."

"I didn't really like him as a boyfriend," Mom explained. "He was a little man and I always felt like a giant next to him. Anyway, I can't like a man who doesn't enjoy eating. He used to make chicken soup for himself by putting two *pulkeys* (drumsticks), a carrot, an onion, and a piece of celery in some water. What kind of a soup is that? And then he told me that he would get two meals out of it because he only eats one drumstick at a time."

My mother was ecstatic when she met Wally. He had all the qualities she was looking for in a man now that she was

Ruth Klein, mother of Syd Lieberman, 1932

seventy. "He's got all his teeth, he likes to eat, and he can
drive at night. He's perfect," she told me.

After five years Mom and Wally decided to get married,
but then Wally developed trouble walking. The doctors
discovered a malignant tumor on his spine. Wally's condition
declined until finally he was confined to a wheelchair. Then
a stroke hospitalized him. I visited him with Mom right after
the stroke. Wally couldn't talk, but from the tears in his eyes
I could tell how happy he was to see her. The whole time
Wally looked at her with pleading eyes. She leaned close,
and turned her ear to his mouth, thinking he would whisper
something. When she did, Wally kissed her on the cheek.
"He kissed me," said my mother, holding her cheek. "He
kissed me." A few weeks later Wally died.

After spending her whole life with men, what would my
seventy-eight-year-old mother do now that she was alone?
"I need a younger man," Mom mused shortly after Wally died.
"Look at the movie stars. They're all marrying younger men.
I don't want some crotchety old guy at this stage of the game.
I want someone who can still get around, who can still see,
who can still eat. Someone who knows how to live."

Then, as if surprised at her own audacity, Mom laughed.
I laughed, too. My mother might be a seventy-eight-year-old
grandmother in a blond wig, but inside danced a saucy teenager
surrounded by boyfriends, a young woman who'd been engaged
to two men at the same time, a showy platinum blond. She was
still a woman who loved men and loved being loved by them.
She'd buried three great loves, but hearing her laugh, I couldn't
help but feel that a fourth might be waiting in the wings.

Lessons by Example

by Susan Siebers

What did I learn from my mother, Elinore Rosenthal Pollay? Among many other things, a love of family, the habit of letter-writing, my fondness for reading, and a strong sense of community responsibility top the list.

My parents married very late in life. Perhaps that's why they appreciated each other so much. In fact, a relative had even offered to knit my mother an afghan if she married, thinking it to be a very safe offer. She had to knit it, though, and my mother thoroughly enjoyed using the afghan, telling its story, and, best of all, being married to my father.

When I went to college, I received daily letters from home. These lasted throughout my college career and beyond. I got my father's letters on Thursdays; on other days, the letters came from my mother. When my son Eli went away to camp, naturally I wrote him the same way.

My mother also inspired me with her enthusiastic ability to lose herself in a good book. One weekend when I came home on a visit from college, she had just completed *The Hobbit* and had started *The Lord of the Rings*. Since I had already read the whole series, I understood immediately why we talked so little that weekend. For a while after that, she even cut the "e" off her name to sign her letters "Elinor," like one of the series' characters.

My mother was a devoted volunteer in *Hadassah* and our local grade school PTA. As a child, I remember standing in the kitchen deciding with great conviction that I would never get involved in organizations. But I somehow forgot that pledge to myself when I joined JRC and all my professional organizations. And, when I became president of JRC in 1977, five years after she died, I realized how my mother had shaped this aspect of my life.

Like the cartoon character Cathy, I am amazed when I realize how much like my mother I am. Unlike Cathy, though, I hope I can continue to emulate her.

My Storybook Stepmother

by Rebecca Rubin

Unlike storybook stepmothers who were wicked and jealous,
my stepmother was like a fairy tale princess who arrived in
a shower of exotica the likes of which I had never seen. Silk
blouses, hats in fancy boxes, perfume, evening gloves, and oil
paintings accompanied my new mother, who also had a wealth
of names—Frieda Louise Merenna Rubin. Few people in the
world that I knew had more than one name, and none of them
were family members. I assumed we couldn't afford the extra
name because we were poor. My father told me that Jewish
people didn't have middle names. This clarification was but a
crumb in the edifice he had constructed to explain our strange
world. That day my world got infinitely brighter because Frieda
came to live with us.

Slim and elegant, she was like no one I had ever seen.
My relatives were loud and pushy on one side; acerbic and
demanding on the other. They all had strange accents, and
strange ideas, and looked uncomfortable in their clothes.
Clearly they were from another world. But Frieda looked to the
manor born. She may have lived in Greenwich Village, but she
shopped on Fifth Avenue—and it showed. She was quiet and
gracious and rarely disagreed. I thought she was absolutely the

most beautiful person I had ever seen. When I now look at photographs from that period, I see that my child's eye was accurate. But looking like Audrey Hepburn's prettier older sister was only part of the total package. Her loving and generous personality so endeared her to me that I have never understood those fairy tale stepmothers.

Frieda Rubin, stepmother of
Bathsheba (right) and Rebecca (front), 1960

Mother

by Judith Blaustein

I didn't call her Mother. I called her Ma or Mom or Mommy,
but I always thought of her as Mother. She wasn't a huggy,
kissy sort of mother, and we never spent an afternoon baking
cookies. But I remember great afternoons painting wildflowers
with her and some wonderful nights lying on our backs and
identifying the constellations.

Unlike other mothers, who let their children win,
Mother's competitiveness made her a great opponent at
games. On *Shabbat* afternoons, she would challenge my
father, brother, and me to play Scrabble "for blood," as she
put it. Each of us would take a book with a bookmark, and,
because we didn't write on *Shabbat,* we would stick the
bookmark in the appropriate page to keep our own scores.
Mother always won. She cared the most about winning.

My mother, Elenora Lily Abeles, was born on the Lower
East Side of New York on Broome Street on February 27,
1909, the last of twelve children. My grandmother was forty-
six years old when Mother was born. She had lost three
children in Hungary before coming to the United States.

When Mother was sixteen, her father died of diphtheria.
At nineteen, Mother became a teacher to support her sixty-

five-year-old mother and herself. Even after marriage and two
children, my mother continued her education, first becoming
an administrator and then getting two additional degrees in
Hebrew education. After retiring, she painted and wrote. While
going through some old boxes in my brother's garage, I found
her account of growing up on the Lower East Side in the early
years of the twentieth century:

> I was born on a wintry Saturday at noon. The only
> heat in our railroad flat came from a black, coal-
> burning stove. The toilet was in the hall. A bathtub
> was made by removing the slate slab between the
> two washtubs. That day, Shabbat, the whole
> family—Papa, Mama, and my eight sisters and
> brothers—sat around a table in the large kitchen.
> Suddenly, my mother felt that I was ready to make
> my entrance. She rushed to the bedroom and sat
> down on the floor to take the baby clothes out of
> the trunk. A few moments later, I was born on the
> bedroom floor. . . .no doctor or midwife. My poor
> father who had spent the morning praying in shul
> had to cut the umbilical cord himself; then he put
> us both to bed.
>
> Although poor in dollars, my family used their
> cents to make sense. My sister Theresa bought
> sweet, over-ripe bananas from a pushcart on her
> way back from work. She got twelve bananas for
> a penny. And my sister Pauline, who came home
> hunched over with lint-covered white hair from her
> hours at a sewing machine, brought us rejected
> jackets from her boss. These were worn by one
> boy and then handed down to a younger brother.

Lily Fankushen, mother of Judith Blaustein, c. 1927

Nowadays, psychologists tell us to touch one another. When I was little, we always did. I slept in the same bed with my sister Charlotte. Once in the middle of the night, she awoke from a dream. She pulled the dangling string overhead and turned on the glare of the room's one bare bulb. "I have to look up the meaning of this dream," she exclaimed, pulling out a half dozen books from under the bed. Charlotte was a romantic. "What could it mean?" Rubbing my half-closed eyes I said, "It means turn out the light and go back to sleep."

*At home we spoke Yiddish-Deutsch, with some
Hungarian, Slovak, and Hebrew phrases thrown in.
On the street, the children spoke Yinglish and I
imitated it. But I knew it wasn't correct English, and
it was one of the first seeds to germinate my lifelong
fascination with language and speech. The teachers
in the public schools made house calls to absentee
pupils. Of course, the family's best china and linen
were used to serve coffee to these honored guests. I
decided to be a teacher.*

*Growing up on the Lower East Side was not easy,
but it was never lonely. We were at home with our
family and friends. We lived not only in huddled,
crowded spaces. We lived in the present time, a link
between the respectfully honored past and the
fervent hope for a better future.*

"When you're pouring, do it over the sink!"

by Eileen Singer Heisler

For Molly Singer, 1921–1981

My husband Marc and I invited two couples to our home to make a complete eight-recipe French feast from *Gourmet Magazine.* Our guests arrived at two o'clock to begin the laborious preparations. Through the long afternoon and evening we used and reused the same pots, pans, and bowls to fulfill each recipe's complex requirements. At one point, we needed to combine a completed sauce with chicken stock, which had just finished cooking on the stove. The chicken stock was hot, and there was a lot of it. To my surprise, I heard myself saying, "When you're pouring, do it over the sink!" It could have been my mother talking.

Growing up in our home, we knew that life wasn't going to be easy. We had no right to expect things to fall into our laps. Life wasn't going to work that way, not for us. We knew that we'd have to work for our rewards and that we'd need plenty of sound advice along the way. Basic, practical, and self-protective advice, not likely to be found in any *Gourmet Magazine* recipe. Advice like "Always pour over the sink." Rest assured Mom, I always do.

Things on a Seder Plate

by Linda Mathias Kaskel

At my grandmother's home, the week before *Pesach* was the most work-intensive week of the year. There were dishes to put away, a special set of dishes to bring out of the basement, and lots of silver to polish. There were cabinets to clean and bags of food to stock for the coming holiday.

I have vivid memories of my grandmother removing her Seder plate from many layers of newspaper. It was one of the few possessions she had brought with her from Germany. Pausing from her housework, she would quiz me on the symbols of the Seder plate: the green *karpas,* representing the new growth of spring; the salt water, representing our sadness and tears; the *maror* and *chazeres,* symbols of bitter slavery; and the roasted shankbone, a symbol of the Passover sacrifice made in the old Holy Temple in Jerusalem. She beamed at me when I showed where her delicious sweet *charoset* went on the plate. I had trouble remembering the last symbol. After a moment, I announced that the egg was the final thing to be placed on the Seder plate. My grandmother smiled and patted my shoulder as we carried the Seder plate to the kitchen.

My first spring in public school, the kindergarten teacher had the class prepare colored eggs, drawing designs on the hard-boiled eggs with white crayons, then dipping the eggs in dye. I was five and had never seen these small works of art. Elated, I drew a six-pointed *Magen David* on my hard-boiled egg and patiently waited my turn for the dye bath. At the end of the day, I placed my precious blue egg into my mitten and then into my coat pocket for safe travel. I slowly walked home, careful not to trip. I was so excited imagining what everyone would say that night when my blue egg appeared on my grandmother's Seder plate.

We arrived at my grandparents' home as the sun approached the horizon. My grandmother and her sister were in the kitchen making last-minute preparations, and the men were in the front room. I crept into the empty dining room and placed my colorful egg next to the roasted egg on the Seder plate.

I then skipped into the kitchen and was quickly shooed out to wash my hands and get ready for candle lighting. A few minutes later, in the dining room, I scanned from one adult face to the next, but no one had noticed my new addition. There was a *new* Seder plate in the middle of the table! I saw the green *karpas,* the salt water, the shank bone, the bitter herbs, the *chazeres,* the *charoset,* and the roasted egg. But my beautiful blue egg was missing. Before I could ask about it, my father nudged me to begin reciting the four questions. I had a fifth question to add to the evening, but whenever I tried to ask it, I was either shushed to be quiet or prodded to sing.

That year, my younger brother was the first to find the hidden *afikomen.* I was searching for my blue egg, not the broken *matzah,* but I turned up empty-handed. Exhausted, I fell asleep sometime after dinner and barely awoke before the final verse of "Who Knows One?" On our way home, I asked my parents about my egg. They did not know what I was talking about. They said I must have dreamed the second egg

and explained that grandmother would never have allowed
such an egg. I knew my egg had been real, but I dismissed the
incident as an unsolved mystery and didn't bring it up again.

Years later, I drove my grandmother to the store for her
Pesach shopping. She carefully inspected each item to insure
that it was Kosher for Passover, explaining to me what was
Kosher and what was *chametz* and could not be used during
the holiday. I finally realized that my dyed egg had not been
Kosher for Passover. Rather than embarrass me, my grandmother had removed the blue egg from the Seder table and
from the house, as Jewish law required.

Now, nearly thirty years later, I am married and have a
daughter. The family Seder is now at our home. The week
before *Pesach,* we polish silver, clean cabinets and take out
the Seder plate. Our Seder plate, a wedding gift from my
grandparents, contains the traditional symbols and a few
newer symbols. There are two types of *charoset*—the mixture
of apples and walnuts and sweet wine that my *Ashkenazi*
relatives have always used, and the mixture of dates and
apricots favored by many *Sephardic* Jews. There is the
roasted beet to honor the symbolism of the Passover sacrifice
without offending the vegetarians at the table. Finally, there
is a round, firm, brightly colored orange to symbolize the
equal participation of women in today's American Jewish
communities.

Out of respect for my grandmother, I never again placed a
non-kosher item on the Seder plate. And I have never removed
a traditional symbol from the Seder plate. It is important to
remember both the Exodus from Egypt and the struggles of
modern American Jews.

Once before my grandmother died, I told her about our
new *Pesach* traditions. She patted my cheek and said it was

Kathinka Mathias, grandmother of Linda Mathias Kaskel, c. 1980

good that I was hosting the Seder and that I should always make my guests feel comfortable. She gave me three secrets of her success: First, cook the carrots for the soup twice as long as the matzah balls. Second, have an extra plate ready for the unexpected guest. Third, never criticize the ideas of your guests or make them feel unwelcome in any way. I would add a fourth: Always answer the questions and honor the contributions of the children who bless your Seder table.

From Russia with Vote

by Maxine H. Lange

My mother, Ruth Gershenoff Horn, was very distrustful of
government. She had lived through a pogrom in her town and
then through the Russian Revolution and its aftermath. The
rest of her family—father, mother, and two sisters—had set
out at different times for America. Left alone, she desperately
wanted to go to the United States. The only possibility was to
enter as a minor since her father was already an American
citizen. But she was older, so she had to lie about her age.

Although she made it here, worked, married and had a
family, she never felt secure. She felt she was living a dangerous
lie. She was sure the powerful U.S. government would discover
her secret and send her back to Russia.

As a widow, many decades later, she needed proof of her
citizenship to obtain a passport. Her important papers had
been lost in a move to Florida. In order to verify when she had
become a citizen, I visited the Cook County Clerk's Office to
check my mother's voting history. There I learned that my
mother's caution about government had not kept her from

Ruth Gershenoff Horn, mother of Maxine H. Lange,
Mogilev, Byelorussia, c. 1920

voting. Records show that she voted in every primary, general, and special election from the date she became eligible. She had never missed an opportunity to cast her precious vote. Maybe she felt it would be protection. Or perhaps she had a special appreciation for this gift.

For Maxine Lange

by Beth Lange & Amy Lange

ON FRIENDSHIP: We called them "Telephone Specials." Back when we were kids, Mom would talk on the phone with friends while making dinner or baking. She had one of those long telephone cords (these were the days before cordless) and she would move about the kitchen chopping, mixing, measuring and talking. (Today this is called multi-tasking). She would invariably leave out ingredients—sometimes incidental ones, but often key ingredients like the leavening for the cake, or the lemon in the lemon bars. Sometimes the omission was the timer, and she would let foods cook to a crisp. We'd joke about these telephone specials and she'd take it in good humor. We learned that the magical ingredient in her telephone specials was her friendships. She taught us that conversations shared over meals are more important than the food. And friendship —keeping in touch, being available, offering support, sharing lives—these are the important ingredients in life.

ON NATURE: Though all nature is to be preserved and respected, one doesn't have to like beetles or bears or mice up close!

ON *TIKKUN OLAM:* From a wee age we were going on civil rights marches, giving *tzedakah,* and stuffing envelopes for one cause or another. There was hardly a time when our mother wasn't sitting on a board, going to a political meeting, supporting a new organization, working on a campaign. She taught us to be involved and take responsibility in our community. When she ran for the Evanston City Council in 1971, we proudly blitzed our neighborhood with her campaign literature, drove around sporting her car-top carrier placard, ran reminders on election day, endured her many absences to attend coffees and campaign door-to-door, stood outside the polling place at the fire station as judges tallied the ballots and reveled in the joy of her victory. We then watched Mom take on causes and champion issues for eight years. She not only modeled for us the importance of *Tikkun Olam*—helping to fix at least our little piece of the world in Evanston—she showed us, often, that it is perfectly acceptable to disagree openly with others and be feisty about it. We recall many a night when she would argue her causes, going head-to-head with those who opposed her, even when some resorted to name-calling. But she remained steadfast in working for what she believed. And she has never stopped championing causes, volunteering her time, speaking on behalf of those with less opportunity or power, and lobbying to make the world more just. Her energy and commitment are daunting.

Clara Halpern, mother of Ruth Gideon, Austria, c. 1921

Sudden Death

by Carol Friedman

My mother has an old black-and-white photograph of her mother. It's small, maybe two by three inches, with scalloped edges. In this picture my grandmother wears a heavy coat trimmed with a thick fur collar. Her face is partially hidden by wire-framed glasses that have slipped slightly down her nose, and a cloth hat pulled down over her dark hair. She has on thick stockings and fashionable pumps with a strap buttoned across her toes. Something—perhaps a fur muff or a twine-wrapped brown paper package—conceals her hands. She stands in front of a shop in Stuttgart, Germany, her birthplace. I scan the photograph for clues about her life, which ended without warning at age thirty-six. But the picture leaves too much unsaid.

Who photographed her that day? Where was she going and where had she been? Does that package conceal a book she had ordered at the bookseller's? Who were her friends? Did she enjoy being the mother of her ten-year-old and five-year-old girls? What did she do with her daughters when they weren't in school or being taken care of by the nursemaid?

As a child, I never ran out of questions about my grandmother, but there were few answers. I didn't even know

Else Löwenstein Dreifus with daughter, Anneliese,
mother of Carol Neubauer Friedman, February 1922, Stuttgart

her real name until I was much older. Mother always referred
to her as "Oma," even though she did not live long enough to
be a grandmother to her six rowdy American grandchildren.
I somehow associated my "Oma" with a white truck whose
faded red lettering advertised "Omar Bakery" as it circled our
neighborhood twice a week delivering donuts, fruit pies, and
cakes to other people's houses.

    None of us was to know this grandmother, who left
home one morning for a minor procedure at the most

renowned women's clinic in the region and never returned. Just about the only good thing anyone can say about the tragic death of this beautiful young woman is that she missed the Holocaust by half a decade and so was spared the grim choice of being chased out of her beloved homeland with the rest of her family or facing extermination. She also never had to see the shattered remains of her parents' home or her family's business appropriated by the Nazis who stormed her hometown (even though Jews like her parents had been assimilated community members for generations, and young men like her brother had given their lives for the Kaiser in the first World War).

No consolation for my mother. No one ever explained anything to her. Early the next morning my grandfather reportedly ushered her and her sister into his study. Without preface, in one curt sentence, declared they would never see their mother again, because she had died unexpectedly overnight. That was all. From then on my mother lived without a mother. Whatever my mother remembered of her mother was either bound up in grief or forgotten forever.

So who was my grandmother? All I get is this tiny photograph, bent in the corner, to suggest a whole personality, a life? Scarred by her own motherless childhood, my mother could not help me understand how I connect to her, to her mother, to all the women who came before. The answers she never heard might have helped her weave together enough threads of her mother's life to save her from the silence of not knowing and of never being able to ask.

"Don't open the door for anyone, no matter what."

by Karen Kaplan

The year was 1959 and I was four years old. My older sisters were both at school, and I was home with my mom. Mom needed an ingredient for a recipe she was cooking, and she ran to a grocery two blocks away, leaving me home alone, knowing she would be back in just a few minutes. Her rules for this situation were direct and concise, and they left no room for interpretation: Do not touch the stove, keep your hands away from the kitchen utensils, and under no circumstances open the door for "anyone."

An independent and self-sufficient child, I happily watched as she faded from sight down the block; then I busied myself with my toys. And then, to my amazement, the doorbell rang. I froze, remembering my mother's instructions. What should I do? I decided to ignore the doorbell. The bell rang again and I got scared. I heard a voice and decided to walk over to the window to see if I could identify the ringer.

It was Grandpa Sam—just about my favorite person on the planet! Grandpa was retired, but he drove a taxicab, and when he was in the neighborhood, he would stop in and visit.

I grabbed the crank for the casement window and opened it enough to say, "Hi Grandpa!"

"Open the door, I need to use the bathroom!" said Grandpa.

"No, Mommy said I can't open the door for anyone, no matter what."

"But I'm your Grandpa, you know me, and I really, really need to use the bathroom."

Samuel Hafer with granddaughters, Karen and Robin Berger, 1959

Again I repeated Mommy's strict instructions. After more pleading, Grandpa reluctantly walked to his cab and drove to a gas station to use the restroom.

When mom returned, just a few minutes later, I related my short conversation with Grandpa. The look on her face showed love and pride but also disappointment—love and pride because she knew she could trust me, but disappointment that her instructions had been severe and unthinking; she could have told me to make an exception should Grandpa happen to be in the neighborhood.

We laughed about the incident many times with Grandpa and other relatives, and I have retained a reputation for being extremely trustworthy and maybe a bit too literal.

Live and Learn

by Freddi Greenberg

My mother's hair lost its color in her twenties. Her concerned mother sought the advice of a doctor. But nothing was wrong. Some sixty years later, my mother's hair is still a beautiful white.

Like her hair color, my mother's other memorable characteristics remain unchanged. She has long been a favorite of my girlfriends, as well as my sisters' friends. Guests to our house have always been able to count on a great piece of chocolate cake. But most of all, my mother has been our lifelong role model. My high school friends labeled her an intellectual because she always wanted to discuss a book or an article she had just read. These friends still stop by to visit with her. And a stack of books, magazines and newspapers still decorates her bedroom.

World War II had interrupted Mom's own college education, but she took a degree-completion program after I went away to school. When my father retired, at my mother's urging, both began attending two to four Northwestern University classes each week. They especially liked eating in the student union along with the other "college kids." After my father's death three years ago, Mom's zeal for learning continued. She kept right on attending Northwestern classes all day, twice a week.

Charlotte Greenberg,
mother of Freddi, 1977

Years ago, Mom advised me to find something that interested me and gave me enjoyment as a cure for my adolescent insecurities. I've been following that advice now for forty years. More importantly, Mom has always taken her own advice. Today she forgets her concerns about fading memory or dimming eyesight as she listens to the symphony, watches a play, or attends her classes. She holds season tickets to two symphonies and two theater companies, and recently cabbed downtown to the Goodman alone when I was unable to join her for our usual Sunday matinee. Mom eagerly listens to the news and never fails to ask about items related to my work or to my husband's. She even took a computer class taught by and for seniors. Mom still loves to eat in the Northwestern cafeteria, too, either with an acquaintance from class or sitting alone and taking in the latest collegiate fashions.

By the way, my mother always sits near the front in school, at the symphony, and at the theater. You'll recognize her by her hair. Stop and say hello. If you're lucky, she may invite you over for that legendary chocolate cake.

The Bridal Gown

by Cheryl Bondy Kaplan

When Mary Helen became engaged to my Uncle Bill in the 1950s, two cultures clashed. Uncle Bill grew up in a Jewish, upper-middle-class Chicago family; Mary Helen grew up Protestant on a farm in a small town in southern Illinois. They met on their first day of art school in Chicago when Mary Helen asked Bill for directions back to her apartment. Despite their different backgrounds, Bill's family embraced Mary Helen.

Mary Helen and her family planned the wedding on a very limited budget. Bill's mother, my Grandma Gert, asked Mary Helen if she could have the pleasure of taking the bride-to-be shopping for her wedding gown. This made Mary Helen a bit nervous. She was trying to be careful about expenses and felt she would be embarrassed if she couldn't afford the gowns at an upscale Chicago salon. So she decided to be direct with Gert and tell her exactly what she could afford to spend on a dress. Not to worry, Gert assured her, they certainly could find a beautiful gown in that price range.

Now Gert was a gorgeous, elegant woman. Until the day she died, she always donned the latest fashions—with matching shoes and handbag. This was not a woman whose idea of a perfect day was making *kreplach* and baking *mandel brot.* After she died, her family would joke that a few exclusive boutiques in her town of Scottsdale, Arizona, probably went belly-up for lack of business. Her passion of shopping for *haute couture* could intimidate even the most sophisticated folks, not to mention a shy young farm girl from Fairfield, Illinois.

The big shopping day came. Gert ushered Mary Helen to a bridal salon, where each dress seemed more beautiful than the one before. Finally, Mary Helen tried on a dress that lit up her face. She crossed her fingers, asked the price and— miracle of miracles—the dress cost exactly what Mary Helen had budgeted. She couldn't believe her good luck! She paid the bill, got married, had three children, and stayed married some forty years until Uncle Bill's death.

Only after many years did the proverbial light bulb click on in Mary Helen's head. How obvious it seemed (in hindsight) that her very generous mother-in-law must have been in cahoots with the salon's saleswoman to quote the budgeted price for any dress, with Gert's promise to cover the balance later. When Mary Helen confronted her on the matter, Gert merely said, "I'll never tell."

Looking Back:

Memories of My Mother

by Sholom Gliksman

My mother was the one constant in my life. It seems that, until her death, she was always a part of my life, the one person who was always there.

Now that she has been gone for over a year, I find myself reviewing what I know of her life—curious in a new way about who she was and what her life was about.

She was born in Ostrog, a small city in Ukraine which had a sizeable Jewish community. Her parents were well-off. She studied nursing and had many friends.

Then came the upheavals. One change after another. My mother's parents and siblings moved to America. My mother married a handsome, young Zionist and together, they made *aliyah* to what was then Palestine. Her husband joined the Jewish *Palmach* underground army and, during the Hebron riots, was killed driving over a mine planted by Arabs. Her dreams shattered, my mother responded to her family's request to join them in the United States.

She traveled via Europe, where she stopped to say good-bye to relatives and friends in the communities where she had lived as a girl. She escaped just before the suspension of civilian travel and the outbreak of the Holocaust, knowing that terrible things were about to happen to her remaining relatives, her friends from childhood, and the world she had grown up in. Eventually, she developed a reading mania for books on the Holocaust, seeking to understand how ordinary Germans and other Europeans could have turned such hatred and violence towards the Jewish people in general, and her extended family and childhood friends in particular. But this was much later.

My mother made it to America—Farmingdale, New Jersey, to be exact. She met and married my father, and moved with him to Detroit, where I was born. Perhaps these were the happiest years of her adult life. She always talked about her love for my father, and I still can recall the joy in her eyes when he would come home from work. But my father had heart trouble. One night, when I was six years old, my father had a major heart attack and died. My mother was once again a widow.

I have always wondered where she found the strength to continue. Her most cherished memories were of people either dead or in worlds far away. She had no one around with whom she could share many memories. I think she must have been terribly lonely. And yet, she didn't allow bitterness to interfere with the business of living. She was able to find joy in new experiences and new friends, in her many organizations, in going to the Covenant Club, in visiting even older people at a nearby nursing home, or in giving a box of candy to the staff at her doctor's office.

My mother taught me a lot. Most of all she taught me to cherish life, even if it is full of adversities.

Mom Worries

by Jonathan Markowitz

I

wonder

if

I

remembered

to

thank

my

mother

enough?

Clean up your room!

Did you do all your homework?

Where are you going tonight?

Do you have enough money?

When will you be home?

Why aren't you eating?

Of course you will have a date.

You look beautiful.

Don't forget to call when you get there.

I love you.

Lenore Markowitz with daughter, Beth and son, Jonathan, 1958

Motherhood and Apple Pie

by Margaret Lurie

My mother was the sister of Admiral Hyman Rickover, father
of the nuclear navy, well-known for his high standards and
sense of discipline. My mother had a lot of the same traits,
but she was running our household, not the U.S. Navy.

It was extremely important to my mother that I learn to be
an organized, disciplined person. Her methods of instilling this
in me may be amusing today but were a real source of conflict
between us then. For example, before I was allowed to leave
for school in the morning, my room and bathroom had to
undergo inspection: bed made perfectly in military fashion,
drawers neat with every item of clothing folded straight, every
surface and corner clean in my bathroom. If not, I had to go
back and redo them. My friends had to wait outside until I
passed muster.

She also believed that it was important to learn how to
cook. But the emphasis was on cooking as a discipline. For
example, my mother taught me as a young girl to make pies,
and she insisted on perfect crusts. No patched-together jobs;
the lattice top had to be perfect before I could go out to play.
Apple pie offered the opportunity for me to peel apples in one
complete spiral—the mark of a true cook, apparently.

Of course, I complained bitterly about these tasks, but they did have the desired effect: a sense of organization and discipline that has remained with me all my life. I also learned that as soon as I could afford it, I would have someone else clean the bathrooms.

I have tried to instill some of this sense of discipline and organization in my children, with mixed results. They seem to understand that life can be easier when you are on top of things. But since I never used my mother's methods, today not one of them can make a perfect pie crust.

Augusta Rickover Berman with daughter, Margaret, 1953

The "Tallis"

by Joan Dumser

My son, my first-born, the most physical image of myself
on this earth, is becoming a Bar Mitzvah. He is enthusiastic
about learning his portion, and he is determined to write a
meaningful *d'var Torah*. He wants to pick out the color of the
invitations and even help decide what food we serve. Every
mother should know such involvement. I am blessed. I am
excited. I am terrified.

I have been a Jew for only seven years. Though I've been
committed to a Jewish life since before my marriage, I was
raised a Roman Catholic. I went to Catholic schools. Together
with my parents and five siblings, I went to mass regularly and
said the rosary after meals and during long car trips.

In the year preceding my son's Bar Mitzvah, I think, plan,
and try to learn everything about being Jewish. About four
months before the event my mother calls. She wants to know
what kind of present is appropriate.

"I was thinking of making him a prayer shawl," she says.
"Will he need that?" In the background I hear my father: He
doesn't need a prayer shawl; he'll get one from his father.
I correct him. "No, Dad. Men are buried in their *talleisim*.

I think it would be wonderful if mom makes a *tallis.*" I'm so
happy when my son thinks it's a great idea, too.

My mother is an excellent seamstress. She knows fabrics
and styles. She's been sewing for over sixty years. In high
school she won a contest for designing and sewing a suit.
The prize was a set of shears in a soft pink leather case about
the size of a loose-leaf binder. This scissors case sat on the
dining room table during every sewing project: matching
dresses for my sisters and me, a suede jacket for my brother,
baby clothes for our children. I see cloth draped over her
hands, the knuckles bulging slightly, her gold wedding band
loose on her finger. My mother making a *tallis* for her Jewish
grandson is exactly right.

I send her instructions on how to make a *tallis* from the
First Jewish Catalog. She sends me fabric samples. She shops
for cloth on 4th Street in Philadelphia, also known as *Shmatta*
Alley. Each of the little storefront shops seems to be owned
by an old Jewish guy and she tells every one of them, "I'm
making a *tallis* for my grandson's Bar Mitzvah." They all give
her advice: It has to be big enough to cover a walking two-
year-old child; you can't mix wool and linen in the same
garment. I picture them bent over in dimly lit stores, perhaps
remembering their own Bar Mitzvahs, wondering why this
woman from the suburbs of New Jersey can't just go to her
temple gift store and buy a *tallis.* They're probably even more
confused when they figure out she isn't Jewish.

My mother is committed to accuracy. She calls regularly
with progress reports and details. Sometimes I feel what she's
asking couldn't possibly be important. Other times I feel I'm a
bad Jew if I don't have an immediate answer; I'm afraid she
thinks I'm just pretending at this religion because I don't know
everything.

Stephanie Dumser, mother of Joan, with grandson,
Zachary Rudin, August 1999

Now it's time to tie the long fringes on the corners of
the *tallis*. On Devon Avenue I buy the strings in a package.
Among the swirl of thick threads is a single blue string that
my mother has specifically requested. "It says that the *tallis*
is supposed to have a blue string in the corner to represent
God's throne." My mother is amazing. I go to the *Jewish*
Book of Why and find that ancient Jews chose the color blue
because of the Mediterranean Sea and because God's throne
is said to be covered in sapphires. But the passage goes on to
say that the blue fringe is not included on a *tallis* any longer
because the special formula for blue dye has been lost and
duplicating the color by artificial means would be improper.
Why then, is there a blue fringe in the packet I pick up from
Rosenblum's? This is a reminder to me that ancient Jewish
scholars may have had too much time on their hands.

My mother reports having trouble with the strings. I tell her to tie them around the slats of a chair. She ties and reties the fringes to get them exactly right. Finally she's done. She asks me if he needs something to carry it in and I think, just like mom—to remember that, too.

The *tallis* arrives in the mail. I unwrap a heavy shirt box covered in brown paper. I push away the tissue paper and see the *tallis,* a creamy white, lightweight wool with bands of green, blue, and gold on opposite ends of the fabric. I hold it in my hands. It's beautiful. And she's made a *tallis* bag to match.

On the day of the Bar Mitzvah, my parents are called up to the *bimah* to present this *tallis* to their grandson. As they walk up the few steps, I think of the months of planning and doing that brought us here together. My mother fumbles slightly while opening it to its full length. I want to jump up and tell everyone that my mother made this; she picked out the material and learned to tie the fringes. I should have told the rabbi how long she worked on it. Surely he would have acknowledged her work. I should have told him that my Catholic mother, who has sewn christening dresses for her other grandchildren, has made a *tallis* for my son, a garment he will use almost daily for years to come.

My mother hands the *tallis* to her grandson and the service continues. But this passing of the cloth from old hands to young is my clearest image of the day.

My Yiddishe Mama

by Barbara Mastoon

I fondly remember my mother of years past. It seems like she
was always ironing mountains of laundry that a husband and
four children would accumulate each and every week. Though
it must have been drudgery, she never complained. In fact, I
recall her singing in her lovely voice while she worked.

My mother often made up words that sounded like Yiddish,
but weren't. Everyone had their own nickname (mine was
Boptzu). We all knew that *chitenayu* meant it was bedtime. As
a result, we acquired a vocabulary of "secret" family words that
we used like a private and affectionate code.

She loved eating candy—jellied green spearmint leaves,
"chicken bones," (a hard candy with a soft, sweet center), and
chocolate-covered orange peels. Occasionally she took some
well-deserved time to relax. It was usually spent enjoying a
good game of mah jongg. I can still hear the tiles clicking
against each other. Wins or losses rarely totaled more than
a dollar—but she was always happy whatever the outcome.

Mom was very proud of her extended family, which
basically included anyone who was Jewish. She beamed
with pride as she told our family that Sandy Koufax thought

enough about his religion that he wouldn't play in the World Series on *Rosh Hashanah.* Conversely, she was so ashamed of the "Son of Sam."

Now I see that very little has changed. Gramma Mollye, as she is known, continues to be a caring wife and mother, as well as a grandmother and great-grandmother. Her conversations are dotted with expressions like "G-d willing" and "take one day at a time" and, of course, all those colorful Yiddish-like words of her own invention.

Mollye Bernstein Friend, mother of Barbara Friend Mastoon, 1950

What We Learned from Our Mother

by Judith Kohn

As our mother grew older, she liked having us tease her about the things we had learned from her. Her eyes would twinkle and her smile grow broader as we laid out her accumulated imparted wisdom. At her seventieth birthday brunch, we presented a list of "Things We Learned from Our Mother." They included:

(1) Always bring a sweater.

(2) Never buy retail if you can help it.
If you can't help it, don't buy.

(3) Never borrow money if you can help it.
If you can't help it see #2, above.

(4) Reciprocate quickly, preferably in kind. If someone invites you for dinner, invite that person back for dinner within a couple of weeks. If someone sends over a batch of cookies, send back a batch of *mandel* bread.

(5) Remember to say thank you. Don't procrastinate. Write thank-you notes. Make thank-you telephone calls. Depending on the situation, send thank-you gifts.

(6) Don't wear white after Labor Day.

(7) Accomplish something every day. Get dressed and get
    your work done early in the day, so you can justify time
    for yourself later.

Our mother, Beatrice Silverman, died last year. On the
day she died, she reminded us to "bring food for everyone."
Confused at the time, we later recognized this admonition as
an extension of the "thank-you" rule.

At the funeral, though, we discovered something else our
mother had taught us: Take the time to show you care. She had
never put that rule into words, but our mother had friends from
her home in Philadelphia, friends in our family, friends from
every neighborhood where she'd lived and every job that she'd
held, and friends who were our friends, too. When she died,
those friends came forward with eloquent notes, photographs,
donations, and long-distance calls, to let us know just how
important our mother had been to them.

The rabbi who spoke at her funeral said that when he visited
our mother in the hospital, she had seemed as interested in him
as he was in her. He found that unusual for someone who was
as ill as she was, someone who might well have been bitter or
despondent. But she had always taken the time to find out what
was on her friends' minds and to offer what she could: her
presence, a meal, a phone call, a card, or a note. She listened.
She remembered. She showed interest. And she was sincere.

Our mother had a gift for caring. She knew what real
caring looked like and what it took to make it felt. So we'll
probably still shop the sales, write thank-you notes, and put
away our white clothes after Labor Day. But we'll also know
the virtues of our mother's style of caring. And that may be the
most important thing we learned from her.

The Person I Admire the Most:

My Mother, Judith Kohn

by Lauren Kohn*

The person I admire the most is my mom. I admire my mom because she is such a great person. Let's take her job. She is an Employee Benefits Manager. What that means is that people come to her who are very sick. She helps them to get a health plan that fits their needs. She always wants to help people. Besides, my mom is always understanding. If I ever do bad in anything, she does not yell or punish me. She knows I tried my best. In fact, my mom will always think of others before herself. If I want to go shopping at Northbrook Court, and she wants to go grocery shopping, she will always take me where I want to go. Furthermore, my mom never gets down on herself. She always was bad at sports, but she doesn't care. Certainly my mom influences me to do good in school. When my mom was little, she was real smart. I want to be like her. My mom never pushes me at anything. Also, my mom is a pushover. That is good. My mom always gives compliments. I love my mom!!!

* Written in 1988 when Lauren was nine years old.

Riva Markelevich Thatch with daughter, Rhoda Kamin, 1950

On Aging with Joy

by Shirley Gould *

I can hardly believe it, the way the numbers keep getting bigger every birthday. We're told in the Torah that life is "three score and ten." I'm now past eighty.

We all know the bad stuff about old age: the illness, the loneliness, the poverty. But there's a lot of really good stuff, too, if one can manage to stick around and enjoy it. For example, time is a real gift of old age. For the first time in my life, I can do what I want when I want to, and if I don't feel like doing anything, that's okay, too. My whole being tenses up if I'm out of the house around three o'clock in the afternoon, until I remind myself that the children won't be coming home from school, expecting me to be there. Similarly, away from home at night, I don't have to hurry back to relieve the baby sitter.

With all this time at my disposal, I can take on new challenges, learn new skills, and take new courses—not for any particular goal, but just because I want to. In the past

* Editor's note: One of our more senior members,
Shirley Gould is a matriarch of our congregation,
and her advice on aging is therefore included here.

Parts of this essay in different forms have appeared in the JRC newsletter;
Sh'ma Periodical; and North Shore Magazine, Senior Edition.

Shirley Gould, 1999

ten years or so, I learned to quilt, I learned to present book reviews in public, and I'm learning to use a computer. In my synagogue, I'm continually learning more about the Torah— how to speak about it and how to chant passages. I've even learned how to lead a service. In fact, one of the great discoveries of my freedom is that learning is more fun than anything!

Nearing the end of a lifetime of prudence with money, I now have the freedom to spend, although lifelong habits are hard to break. I still compare prices and quantities for everything from groceries to vitamins, and I'm stingy about spending money on such frivolities as cosmetics and hair-dressers. I keep telling myself that I don't have to save for my old age; I'm there already. I don't have to be concerned about saving up for a home or paying for college—my husband and I did that already, several times over.

In the California retirement community where my brother lives, they say they don't buy green bananas. I do. They ripen fast enough. And there's always somebody around to eat them, even if I won't be. They have another saying there that if you wake up in the morning, and it hurts all over, you know you're alive. I think of that one when the arthritis pains make it difficult to get up and move around. Happens often.

There aren't many role models for a vibrant old age. I've been searching for quite a while. But, as I've done many times in my life, I'm plugging away at it, making the most of whatever time there is left to me, focusing on growing rather than standing still, and thanking the Power for each day that I awaken to enjoy. I've been told that I should be thankful continually for my good fortune, and I certainly am.

Getting older makes me think of many long streetcar rides when I was a child, often alone. The rides were full of unexpected stops and starts, twists and turns, but eventually I would arrive. The ride I'm on now, toward death, happens only once. I don't know how long it will be or where the destination is, but I'm not asking, "Are we there yet?" because I'm pretty sure I'll know.

Glossary

afikomen traditionally, a piece of matzah which is broken at the beginning of a Passover Seder and becomes the final food or "dessert" eaten at a Seder meal

aliyah literally *going up;* typically meaning the act of moving to Israel or the honor of being called to the Torah

Ashkenazi(m) Jews whose ancestors lived in Western Europe or former Soviet Union

Bar Mitzvah literally *son of the commandment;* usually understood as a ceremony in which thirteen-year-old boy becomes a full participant in the adult Jewish community; the analogous female ceremony is the **Bat Mitzvah**

bimah raised platform, or stage from which services are led

bris ritual circumcision held on the eighth day after birth of a boy

chai *life,* in Hebrew; each Hebrew letter has a numerical equivalent and the letters that spell the word *chai* equals eighteen and is associated with good luck

challah braided bread traditionally eaten on Sabbath and holidays

chametz food which is leavened and ritually unfit for Passover

charoset a fruit, wine, and nut mixture used as part of a Passover seder to symbolize mortar used to make bricks in Egypt

chazeres (chazeret) a bitter herb used in addition to the maror as part of a Passover seder

d'var Torah an explication of a section from the Torah

emunah faith, belief

gefilte fish stewed or baked fish stuffed with a mixture of the fish flesh, bread crumbs, eggs, and seasoning; prepared as balls or oval cakes boiled in a fish stock

genug enough

Hadassah a Zionist organization of Jewish women devoted to a variety of social and health related causes in Israel and the Diaspora

karpas a leafy vegetable symbolizing spring, used as part of a Passover seder

kiddush sanctification or blessing of the Sabbath and holidays, recited over wine

kippah (pl. **kippot**) head covering which shows piety

klezmer a type of traditional Jewish music from eastern Europe

kreplach noodle stuffed with spiced meat and served in soup

kvell beam with pride

Magen David star or shield of David; a six pointed Jewish star

mandel brot, mandel bread hard cookie-like pastry made with ground almonds

maror a bitter herb used as part of a Passover seder to symbolize slavery

maven expert

matzah, matzoh unleavened bread eaten during Passover

mitzvah a religious commandment or good deed

Kay Patrell, mother of Mel Patrell Furman, c. 1940

nudnik someone who annoys or bothers people, a pest

Palmach an elite fighting force of the *Haganah,* the Jewish army of Palestine which became the Israeli Defense Forces after 1948

Pesach the holiday that celebrates the deliverance of the Jews from slavery in Egypt; also called **Passover**

Pirkei Avot *Lessons from our Fathers* or *Ancestors;* a classical Jewish text from the Talmud containing ethical teachings

pogrom attacks on Jewish population of Eastern Europe and former Soviet Union often condoned or organized by local authorities

Rosh Hashana two day Jewish New Year holiday usually occurring in September; part of the "Days of Awe" or High Holy Days which are followed ten days later by Yom Kippur

schmear a smear of cream cheese on a bagel; spread

seder literally *order;* ceremonial meal held at beginning of Passover

Sephardic, Sephardim Jews whose ancestors lived in Spain, parts of central Europe, northern Africa and parts of Middle East

shabbes, shabbos, shabbat Jewish Sabbath which lasts from sunset on Friday until nightfall Saturday

shmatta rag

shul synagogue

shtetl village or small town in Eastern Europe where many Jews lived before World War II

Torah The Five Books of Moses

tallis (pl. **talleisim**), **tallit** (pl. **tallitot**) prayer shawl with ritual fringes

Tikkun Olam repair of the world

trayf unkosher food, often non-kosher meat

Anna Uretz Dintzis,
mother of Gerry Salzman,
high school graduation, 1912

tzedakah charity given as a religious obligation

Yiddish language spoken by Jews of eastern Europe

Yiddishkeit Yiddish (eastern European Jewish) culture

Yinglish a combination of Yiddish and English

Zionist one who supports the establishment and maintenance of a Jewish state in the land of Israel

Order Form

To order additional copies of *Pirkei Imahot: A Celebration of Our Mothers,* copy this page (your mother wouldn't want you to tear pages out of books!) and fill out the form below.

Please make checks or money orders payable to JRC, and allow up to three weeks for delivery.

1–9 books:

_____ x $14.95 plus $5 shipping & handling* = $_____

10–19 books:

_____ x $12.95 plus $7.50 shipping & handling* = $_____

20 or more books:

_____ x $9.95 plus $10 shipping & handling* = $_____

Ship to:

Name: _____

Address: _____

_____

City: _____

State: _____ Zip Code: _____

Phone: _____ Email: _____

Mail your check and order to:

Pirkei Imahot, c/o JRC

303 Dodge Avenue, Evanston, IL 60202

* sent to a single address